Thomas Llewellyn

Tracts, Historical and Critical

Thomas Llewellyn

Tracts, Historical and Critical

ISBN/EAN: 9783744641173

Printed in Europe, USA, Canada, Australia, Japan

Cover: Foto ©Lupo / pixelio.de

More available books at **www.hansebooks.com**

TRACTS,

HISTORICAL

AND

CRITICAL.

By the late THOMAS LLEWELYN, LL. D.

SHREWSBURY:
PRINTED AND SOLD BY J. AND W. EDDOWES.
SOLD ALSO BY RIVINGTON AND LONGMAN, LONDON;
FLETCHER, OXFORD; MERRILL, CAMBRIDGE;
MARSH, WREXHAM; POOLE AND
BROSTER, CHESTER; AND
RODEN, DENBIGH.

1793.
[PRICE FOUR SHILLINGS AND SIXPENCE, IN BOARDS.]

DEDICATION.

To the Right Reverend

J O H N,

Lord BISHOP of BANGOR.

My Lord,

WHAT fuggefted to me the idea of republifhing the fubfequent Tracts, was the appearance of a Folio impreffion of the Welfh Bible, that iffued from the Clarendon prefs in Oxford, at the clofe of the year 1789.

Refpecting a work of fuch magnitude and importance, it will naturally be inquired,

quired, who were the original promoters of it. When therefore it shall be known, that to Your Lordship's exertion and liberality Wales is entirely indebted for this very seasonable supply to her Churches; I dare appeal to the Publick in general, and to my Countrymen in particular, whether I should be excusable in ushering into the world a republication of this nature, without recommending it to Your Lordship's favour and patronage.

From the high sense of obligation the Author himself entertained towards the benefactors of his Country, and from the strain of gratitude in which he speaks of them, I am fully persuaded, that, were he now alive,* he would be among the

* He died in London, in the month of August, 1783.

the firſt to beſtow upon Your Lordſhip a diſtinguiſhed tribute of applauſe.

And as one, who hath much at heart the real intereſt of his Country, and the preſervation of it's Language, to both which Your Lordſhip hath done eminent ſervices, I am equally ambitious of publickly expreſſing the reſpect and gratitude, with which I have the honour to be,

My Lord,

Your Lordſhip's

Moſt humble and dutiful ſervant,

THE EDITOR.

THE CONTENTS.

AN Historical Account of the British or Welsh Versions and Editions of the Bible. With an Appendix, containing the Dedications prefixed to the first Impressions. Page 1 — 117.

Historical and Critical Remarks on the British Tongue, and it's Connection with other Languages, founded on it's State in the Welsh Bible. 119 — 247.

AN
HISTORICAL ACCOUNT
OF THE
BRITISH OR WELSH
VERSIONS AND EDITIONS
OF THE
BIBLE.
WITH AN
APPENDIX,
Containing the DEDICATIONS prefixed to the firſt
Impreſſions.

Pro Patriâ.

PRINTED FIRST IN THE YEAR 1768.

ADVERTISEMENT.

IT will appear from the following account, that it is frequently impossible to procure Bibles for Proteſtants in Wales; and that this has been the caſe more or leſs ever ſince the Reformation; in which time the years of ſcarcity have been many more than the years of plenty. Were this ſufficiently known, it would not remain long (it is apprehended) without a remedy; eſpecially if an objection to ſuch a remedy, ariſing from imagined inconveniencies, attending the preſervation of the Welſh tongue, could be removed.

To inform the publick of this caſe, and to remove this objection, was therefore the firſt and principal intention of the author. He will own himſelf much miſtaken, miftaken, or the objection is here fhown to be, in general, very trifling to the inhabitants either of England or Wales. The prefent was thought a fit feafon for an attempt of this kind; *as the Society for promoting Chriftian Knowledge are now foliciting the affiftance of the able and the generous for the republication of the Welfh Bible.** This firft and principal intention, it is believed, will need no apology. It

* In the Year 1769, the *Society* printed an octavo edition of the Welfh Bible, confifting of 20,000 copies. Of that impreffion they have not at prefent one remaining in their hands; in confequence of which they have it in contemplation to give out propofals for a new one; — what will be very defirable in various parts of the Principality in general. And here the editor feels it a duty peculiarly incumbent on him to record, that the publick-fpirited Prelate, to whom thefe fheets are addreffed, purchafed of the Society, within thefe few years, their laft remaining ftock, amounting to *two thoufand* copies, which his Lordfhip diftributed throughout the diocefe of Bangor; — many of them *gratis*, and the reft at a confiderably reduced price.

" To

It needs none to the writer's own mind. It will need none to the friends of religion, of virtue, and of knowledge;— none therefore to any perfon, whofe approbation is worth having.

The beft way of conveying information of the above cafe was thought to be by an hiftorical deduction of the verfions and editions of the book. But here materials were very deficient. The tranflation

" To thofe clergymen, who are not already members of the above-mentioned *Society for promoting Chriftian Knowledge*, and whofe circumftances will allow it, I would earneftly recommend their becoming fo without delay. The expence is trifling; the ufe may be great. The diftribution of [BIBLES, and] the little religious tracts belonging to the Society, will in fome meafure fupply the want of what I fear is too much difufed amongft us,—*perfonal conference* with our parifhioners. Proper information concerning the mode and terms of admiffion may be had by writing to the Rev. Dr. *Gafkin, Secretary to the Society, in Bartlett's Buildings, Holborn,* London."

See Bp. Porteus's Letter to the Clergy of the Diocefe of Chefter, in 1781.

tion had been made near two hundred years ago. No hiftory had ever been given of this fubject. It was, perhaps, never confidered as important enough to deferve it. It might be deemed fufficient that there was a tranflation; and provided that was well done, no matter when, or by whom. If the editions of the book had been as regular and plentiful, as the verfion is good, the hiftory of them would have ftill remained unattempted; and the want of it would not have had weight enough to prefs the author to this fervice, or to trouble others in this way. If the hiftory feem defective, let it's novelty, let the diftance of the event, let the fewnefs and fcattered condition of the materials, be it's apology. If the manner of it's execution be faulty, the writer alone is to blame. But he has no great notion of multiplying apologies; and is of opinion, that any part of this, and of every other work, which cannot ftand without *propping*, fhould even be fuffered to fall.

He

He has no claim to the Appendix, but that of an editor; nor any right to that, except the right of occupancy. He profeſſes a great regard for the memory of the original proprietors; and would be glad to do them honour by publiſhing any of their remains,* which may have that tendency; more eſpecially in the preſent caſe, ſince theſe their remains may be conſidered as vouchers for the hiſtory; and alſo agreeable to the reader, for their antiquity or curioſity.

* The Editor has in his poſſeſſion a few original letters, written by the Venerable tranſlators of the Bible into Welſh; which, from the nature of their contents, are reſerved for a miſcellaneous publication.

The reader is intreated to correct the following errata.

Page. Line.
2   4 For above-mentioned, *read* laſt-mentioned.
11   (m) For p. 407, *read* p. 310.
14   2 *Read,* unfortunately to be done by *Nobody.*
16   11 *Read,* Act for Uniformity.
19   14 *Read,* uſefulneſs and neceſſity.
21   22 *Read,* aſſociates or aſſiſtants.
73   penult. For of ſome conſequence, *read,* of conſequence.
91   20 For Was, *read,* Were.
106 19 *Read,* eadem ſunt.
108 12 *Read,* quam quis ignorat, uſum, dulc.
109 1—7 *Eraſe* the parentheſis, and place commas.
Ibid. 9 *Read,* in poſterum.
115 (f) *Read,* τὰ παλαιὰ.
124 1 *Read,* indebted.
127 22 *Read,* inferiour.
171 6 *Place, th* in the, in the line below, oppoſite ƃ
185 19 For tripto-tes, *read,* triptotes.
223 10 For participle, *read,* participial.
228 16 *Read,* ϲυνταξις.
234 11 *Read,* ᾿ιϛι.

AN

HISTORICAL· ACCOUNT

OF THE

BRITISH, &c.

THE vulgar verſions of the Bible are in general owing to the Reformation from Popery, and were made either in the ſixteenth century or ſince; an inquiry therefore of this kind is bounded by that important event, and can reach no further back than the reigns of Elizabeth, of Edward the Sixth, or at moſt of Henry the Eighth.

FROM an epiſtle of the Biſhop of St. David (a), prefixed to the Welſh New Teſtament

(a) Dr. Richard Davies.

Teftament printed in 1567 we learn, that there was a Britifh manufcript verfion of the Pentateuch extant in the reign of the laſt-mentioned King. 'I remember,' fays the Bifhop, 'to have 'feen, when a lad, a tranflation of the 'five books of Mofes in the Britifh or 'Welfh tongue, in the poffeffion of a 'learned gentleman, a near relation of 'our family.'

IF we fuppofe the author to be fixty years of age, at the time of writing this epiftle (b); and if we deduct from the date of it forty years, in order to bring us to the time to which he refers; we fhall find that the above verfion muft have been feen as early as 1527, about the middle of the reign of Henry the Eighth, and muft have been made fome time fooner. It was extant therefore a confiderable time before the printing of any part of the Bible in Welfh, and even prior to any printed edition of it

in

(b) He was fixty fix, Le Neve, Faft, Anglic. p. 514.

in Englifh. It is not faid who was the author of this ancient verfion, and there may be no ufe or end of conjecturing; I cannot however forbear obferving that Tyndal, the firft Proteftant tranflator of the Bible into Englifh, was a native of Wales, and lived about this time.

Some other fmall and detached paffages of Scripture feem to have been tranflated into this language, in the days of Edward the Sixth, and printed probably for the ufe of his liturgy or fervice book. One little thing of this fort was publifhed in 1551, in that King's reign, and is mentioned by the late Mr. J. Ames, Secretary to the Antiquarian Society. The title of it, as printed (c) in Ames, is extremely incorrect; it fignifies, in my way of reading it, *Certain portions of Scripture*, perhaps the epiftles and gofpels, *appointed to be read in churches in the time of communion and publick worſhip*, &c. by *W. S.*

(c) Typograph. Antiq. p. 272.

This, little and inconsiderable as it may be thought, seems to have been all the effect the Reformation had in this way, on that part of the kingdom, till the reign of Queen Elizabeth; but that promised and produced something more considerable.

In the year 1562, rather 1563, it was enacted by Parliament (d),

'That the Bible, consisting of the
' New Testament and the Old, together
' with the Book of Common Prayer and
' the Administration of the Sacraments,
' should be translated into the British
' or Welsh tongue; should be viewed,
' perused, and allowed by the Bishops
' of St. Asaph, Bangor, St. David,
' Landaff and Hereford; should be
' printed and used in the churches by
' the first of March in the year 1566,
' under a penalty, in case of failure,
' of forty pounds to be levied on each
' of the above Bishops.

' That

(d) 5 Eliz. c. 28.

VERSIONS OF THE BIBLE.

' That one printed copy at leaſt of
' this tranſlation ſhould be had for and
' in every cathedral, collegiate, and
' pariſh church, and chapel of eaſe,
' throughout Wales, to be read by the
' clergy in time of divine ſervice, and
' at other times for the benefit and
' peruſal of any who had a mind to go
' to church for that purpoſe.

' That, till this verſion of the Bible
' and Book of Common Prayer ſhould
' be completed and publiſhed, the Clergy
' of that country ſhould read, in time
' of publick worſhip, the Epiſtles and
' Goſpels, the Lord's Prayer, the Ar-
' ticles of the Chriſtian Faith, the
' Litany, and ſuch other parts of the
' Common Prayer Book in the Welſh
' tongue, as ſhould be directed and
' appointed by the above-mentioned
' Biſhops.' And,

' That not only during this interval,
' but for ever after, Engliſh Bibles and
' Common Prayer Books ſhould be had
' and remain in every church and chapel
' throughout that country.'

In what manner the latter part of this Statute has been complied with, is not my bufinefs now to inquire. As to the former part, one year after the time, fixed by Parliament, *The New Teſtament, tranſlated into the Britiſh tongue, was printed in a handſome quarto of* 399 *leaves; in black letter as it is called; diſpoſed and divided, as to books and chapters, like our preſent Teſtaments; with arguments and contents to each book and to each chapter; with explanations of difficult words in the margin, but no references to parallel paſſages, as indeed there could not be, for there is no diſtinction of verſes, except in ſome books towards the latter end; which is the more remarkable, as Engliſh editions of the Bible, before this time, have in general that diſtinction.*

OF this verſion the book of the Revelation was tranſlated by T. H. C. M. (e) perhaps Thomas Huet, Chantor or Precentor of Menew, that is, St. David.

(e) Rev. begin. Marg. of this Teſt.

David (f). The second epistle to Timothy, the epistle to the Hebrews, the epistle of St. James, and both the epistles of St. Peter, were translated by D. R. D. M. that is, Dr. Richard Davies, Menevensis, or Bishop of St. David (g). All the rest of this translation was the work of W. S. that is, William Salesbury (h), very eminent, in his day, and amongst his own nation, for his great industry, learning and piety.

THIS Testament was printed in London, in the year 1567, by Henry Denham, at the costs and charges of Humphrey Toy (i). To it is prefixed a Calendar and an English dedication ' To the most virtuous and noble *Prince* Elizabeth, &c.' by the principal translator; and a long epistle in Welsh to his countrymen by the Bishop of St. David.

(f) Le Neve. Fast. Anglic. p. 515.
(g) Marg. Note in this Test. begin. of Epist. to Heb.
(h) 1 John begin. 2 Tim. begin. 2 Thess. end.
(i) Test. itself, at the end.

David. From thefe two pieces and the title-page we underftand, that this verfion was made from the Greek collated with the Latin; that it was made with fidelity and diligence; and that Salefbury had the overfight of the whole, efpecially of the publication, 'by the appoint-' ment,' as he fays, ' of our moft ' vigilant Paftours the Bifhops of Wales.'

But there was no edition, or verfion of The Old Teftament into the Britifh tongue, till above twenty years after this publication of the New. This muft feem extraordinary; and we cannot but be furprifed at fuch a delay, at fuch an inftance of non-compliance with an Act of Parliament.

For the honour of the Bifhops of that time in Wales I would hope, and from an expreffion ufed by Salefbury above I might conclude, that this delay did not proceed from any want of difpofition in them to promote and forward this good, this neceffary work. For the credit of my country I would hope, and

VERSIONS OF THE BIBLE.

and from the little I know of the hiſtory of that period I believe, that this delay did not proceed from want of perſons of ſkill and ability, at that time among the Welſh, to undertake and execute a work of this kind. And for the honour of ſtill greater folks I could wiſh ſuch a non-compliance may not have proceeded from want of ſufficient time allowed, or from any other want of proper and neceſſary proviſion made, for the due and timely execution of it.

I have however ſome ſuſpicions that all here was not as it ought to have been, and let it affect whom it may, I ſhall lay my ſuſpicions before the Reader; and as this will be done with ſubmiſſion to the judgment of others, and with due deference to all proper Authority, it is preſumed I ſhall neither deſerve nor incur blame.

Not to inſiſt on the peculiarity of appointing, for the examination and peruſal of this verſion, five gentlemen, who were to do it, in virtue of their offices;

offices; who may have often, if not generally, been all Englifh, but perhaps were never all together Welfh, or mafters of the Welfh Language: not to infift, I fay, on this very peculiar appointment; my firft doubt refpects the *time*, allowed by the Statute for undertaking and completing this bufinefs. This was between three and four years.

THE tranflating and printing of the whole of Luther's German Bible took up from 1522 to 1532 (k).

THE tranflators of the above mentioned Britifh New Teftament affure us, that it was done with *diligence*, that is, with all expedition poffible; yet it was not finifhed and publifhed, in lefs than four or five years' time.

THE Englifh Tranflation of what is called Parker's, or the Bifhop's Bible, was begun in 1559; but it was not finifhed till 1568. Bifhop Burnet fays indeed that it was printed in 1561. But that is a miftake, as may be known from

(k) Le Long. Biblioth. Sac. vol. ii. p. 201.

VERSIONS OF THE BIBLE.

from Lewis's Hiftory of the Tranflations of the Bible into Englifh (l). And

KING James's new verfion of the Englifh Bible was ordered as early as 1604; but it was not completed and publifhed till 1613 (m).

BOTH thefe verfions, it fhould be remembered, were not, properly fpeaking, new tranflations, but only revifions or corrections of former verfions; yet they took up each of them (as did alfo Luther's) nine or ten years, ere they were completed. But according to the above Statute, The whole Bible, confifting of the New Teftament and the Old, and very probably the Apocrypha, together with the Book of Common Prayer and the Adminiftration of the Sacraments, is to be tranflated for the firft time into the Britifh or Welfh Tongue; is to be viewed and perufed by five different perfons; is to be

(l) Lewis's Hift. of Engl. Tranf. p. 240.
(m) Ibid. p. ~~407~~ 310.

be printed, to be bound, and to be fet up in every church in the country, in the fpace of four, if not of three years.

In this prefent Century, the bare printing of the Bible in that language has taken up as much, if not more time. The edition of 1746 was begun in 1743; and the edition of 1718 was fet about in 1714.

Suppose the time allowed by the Statute to have been fufficient for the purpofe; I fufpect there are here *other omiſſions* or *neglects* of feveral things neceſſary for accomplifhing this bufinefs; which neglects or omiffions might not only have thus procraftinated and deferred it, but have even prevented it's being effected.

For the due performance of our Englifh verfions, with care and expedition, a regular plan is laid down, —the whole Bible is divided into feveral portions; a certain number of perfons, almoft a Septuagint, of known learning and abilities, are appointed by name

to

to undertake and execute the work; their table and other neceffary expences, while employed (eftimated at above One Thoufand Marks, near Seven Hundred Pounds (n); the table, I fay, and other neceffary expences of thefe tranflators are defrayed by the Publick; and from the beginning orders are iffued out by His Majefty, that they be fpeedily and amply rewarded with the firft Parfonages, Prebends, or other goodly Livings, which fhould become vacant (o). But here no fuch provifion is made. Nothing of this kind feems to have been thought of. No royal mandates are iffued out. No care taken for rewarding or fupporting the perfons employed. No divifion of Scripture or parcelling it out among a certain number of perfons. No plan at all laid down. No appointment of any one perfon to undertake the whole or any Part of it. It is
ordered,

(n) Wilkins, Concil. Mag. Brit. vol. iv. p. 408.
(o) Ibid. p. 407.

ordered,—it is ordered to be done, but unfortunately to be done by *Nobody*.

It may be faid, that thefe things are left to the care and direction of the Welfh Bifhops, and ought to have been provided and regulated by them. *They are*, fays the Statute, for the foul's health of the flocks committed to their charge, *to take fuch Order among themfelves*, that this may be done; that is, They are to meet and confult together, They are to nominate and appoint proper perfons to undertake this affair, They are to require and enjoin them to do it, They are to view and perufe the tranflation, when it is done; and if it appears to be right, they are to approve and allow it, and then get it put to the prefs and publifhed. But,

It fhould be confidered, with what fund and at whofe expence all this is to be accomplifhed. How are the Bifhops to engage and prevail upon able and fufficient perfons to undertake it? How are the tranflators to be maintained and

and fupported, while they are employed? Or, How are they to be paid and rewarded afterwards? Who is to defray the expence of the prefs and publication, and other expences neceffarily to be incurred, before the Book can be ready for the ufe of the Publick?

It fhould be remembered likewife, what is the penalty to be inflicted on the Bifhops, in cafe they did not choofe to do all, or any of thefe things. Is it Degradation? Is it Deprivation of their Livings? Is it the Lofs of their Eftates, or any confiderable part of their Property? No. It is no fuch thing. It is a fmall, a trifling penalty. It is a fine of Forty Pounds each, which they muft pay in cafe of non-performance. And what muft be the confequence of performing what is enacted? Why, a much greater Sum expended, which, for ought appears to the contrary, muft all come out of their own pockets.

Suppose any five perfons, at this day in the Kingdom, required by the greateft
Authority

Authority on earth to fee any thing executed of a fimilar kind, or *to take fuch Order among themfelves*, that fuch a thing may be done, or elfe to forfeit Forty Pounds apiece;—would they not much fooner lay down their forfeit money, than engage in an affair, which would coft each of them fome Hundreds? Juft a century from this time, when the prefent Statute came to be re-enacted by the Act of Uniformity with a particular view to the Book of Common Prayer; this claufe of the penalty was wholly omitted as inadequate, improper, or trifling.

WHEN I confider thefe things, my wonder ceafes at the delay in this cafe; and I am almoft tempted to afcribe the verfion and publication of the Bible in the language of Wales,—not to the authority or efficacy of the Statute, in that cafe made and provided, but to the good difpofition, to the generofity, to the zeal and activity of particular, of private perfons.

Two

VERSIONS OF THE BIBLE.

Two or three of thefe worthy patriots and benefactors to their country have been named already. The firft of thefe, Huet, is only guefled at, and little known. 'Davies was a confeffor
'and an exile for his religion, in the
'reign of Queen Mary; he was reftored
'to his country on the acceffion of
'Queen Elizabeth, and made fuc-
'ceffively Bifhop of St. Afaph and St.
'David (p). Salefbury was a private
'gentleman of an eminent family in
'Denbighfhire, of liberal education, for
'a time at the Univerfity, then at fome
'of the Inns of Court near London;
'author of feveral treatifes in Welfh
'and for promoting that language;
'much meriting, fays Wood, of the
'church and of the Britifh tongue (q).'

THE next perfon concerned, in doing his country and the church this fignal fervice, was William Morgan, D. D. Vicar

---

(p) Wood Athen. Oxon. vol. 1. p. 202.
(q) Ibid. vol. 1. p. 153.

Vicar of Llann Rhaiadr in Denbighſhire, promoted in 1595 to the See of Landaff, tranſlated to St. Aſaph in 1601, and in 1604 to a better place. This gentleman for the firſt time ſince the Reformation tranſlated, at leaſt had the principal hand in tranſlating, the whole Old Teſtament, and alſo the Apocrypha, into Welſh; he likewiſe reviſed and corrected the former verſion of the New Teſtament, and had them well and handſomely printed together, by Chriſtopher and Robert Barker, in the *ever memorable year* of 1588. One copy of this book he preſented to the Dean and Chapter of Weſtminſter, in return for the civilities which he had received from that Learned Body, particularly from Dean Goodman. It yet remains in their Library. *It is printed in folio and on black letter; it contains the Old Teſtament, the Apocrypha, and the New Teſtament; it has contents prefixed to each chapter; it is diſtinguiſhed into verſes throughout; it has ſome marginal references; has prefixed*

fixed to it a Latin dedication to Queen Elizabeth; has a calendar, one or two tables besides; and, like the preceding Testament, it is numbered not by pages, but by leaves, which amount to 555.

How Morgan came to undertake this business doth not appear. He doth not seem to have been employed in it by Authority. He doth not seem to have been nominated by the Bishops, commissioners for this affair. It should rather seem, that he engaged in it spontaneously, or influenced only by the usefulness and necessity of the work, and by the wishes and prayers of the good people of the land. This may be inferred, I presume, from the preface or dedication to his Bible. He is quite silent as to any order or injunction upon him, for this purpose; he says nothing of his being appointed by the Bishops his superiors, as Salesbury does in his dedication to the Queen.

It doth not appear when, that is, in what year, he undertook and set about this

this tranflation. We have no reafon to think, that he began foon after the enacting of Queen Elizabeth's Statute, or that he fet out with the tranflators of the New Teftament. It is probable, that he had done nothing about it, till a long while after the publication of their verfion. He had not done much, if any thing, in it, before Whitgift was made Archbifhop of Canterbury. This I infer from the above dedication. He would have funk, he fays, under his difficulties and difcouragements; he would have thrown up and relinquifhed the whole; or he would have brought to the prefs and publifhed only the five Books of Mofes, had it not been for the Archbifhop's fupport and encouragement. This is not the language of a perfon, retained and employed by men in power. It is the language of one who had engaged himfelf freely, and who had it in his own option to perfevere or not. And it fhows too, that he had not done much before 1583, when Whitgift was promoted to Lambeth.

NEITHER

NEITHER doth it fully appear, what affiftance or affociates he had in this work. It may feem an undertaking, too laborious and tedious for one man. Three perfons were employed in tranflating the New Teftament, though fome parts of that had been tranflated before; I mean the Epiftles and Gofpels, printed in Edward the Sixth's reign, which very probably were incorporated into the firft edition of the Teftament, and perhaps may be *the part of it, undiftinguifhed by verfes.* The Old Teftament has the Apocrypha connected with it; by itfelf it is a much larger book; and the original language of it is lefs generally underftood. The tranflation of it muft be a work of more time and difficulty. It is probable therefore, that Morgan was only a Principal in this bufinefs, to whom others fhould be added as affociates or affiftants. But who thefe affiftants were may not be fully known; and it is ftill lefs known, what they did.

WOOD

Wood tells us (r), that he was aided by Dr. Rd. Parry, afterwards Bifhop of St. Afaph. But that I imagine to be a miftake, occafioned by the part Parry acted, above thirty years after, on a fecond verfion or edition of the Welfh Bible. However that be, Morgan himfelf fays nothing of Parry; tho' he has taken care to mention and to make due acknowledgements to feveral gentlemen, his worthy patrons or affiftants. Thefe were the Archbifhop of Canterbury before named; the Bifhops of St. Afaph and Bangor (Dr. Hughes and Dr. Bellot I fuppofe) Dr. Gabriel Goodman, Dean of Weftminfter; Dr. David Powel, a Dignitary, fays Wood, in one of the Cathedrals in Wales (s); Mr. Edmund Pryfe, Archdeacon of Merioneth, author of the Welfh Pfalms in metre; and Mr. Rd. Vaughan, Rector then of Lutterworth, afterwards Bifhop of Bangor, of Chefter, and of London.

THESE

(r) Athen. Oxon. vol. 1. p. 727.
(s) Ibid. vol. 1. p. 245.

THESE gentlemen encouraged and supported our tranflator in his work; they abetted and affifted him; *opem tulerunt*, fays he, *non contemnendam*. They granted him free accefs to their libraries, which muft be of confiderable advantage. They perufed and examined his verfion. They revifed and corrected it for him. While attending the prefs, he lived with the Dean of Weftminfter; *qui*, as he tells us, *relegenti mihi ita adfuit affiduus, ut et labore et confilio me plurimùm adjuverit.* Thefe particulars are known from Morgan's dedication of his book, where he makes the moft honourable mention of his chief patrons and affociates. One would have expected to fee, in this lift, the name of Salefbury; perhaps he was dead by this time, as was alfo Bifhop Davies. Dr. John Davies, we know, had fome hand in this verfion. And fo might fome other perfons, whofe names, for reafons unknown to us, may not have been here inferted.

THUS,

Thus, after a long delay of near thirty years, was the Holy Bible tranflated into the Britifh or Welfh tongue; thus it was printed and publifhed for the firft time in that language, and the intention of the Statute, enacted for that purpofe, at length accomplifhed; which intention after all makes no provifion, but for places of publick worfhip, but for the chapels and churches throughout Wales. A very fcanty, a very poor provifion furely for a Reformed, a Proteftant country. It provides only for the church, that is, for one houfe in a parifh, and that a houfe hardly ever frequented by all the inhabitants, and, in common, not frequented above once in a week by any of them.

How far the prefent publication proved an adequate fupply, even in this refpect, may be doubtful; and cannot be precifely determined, without knowing the number of places, appropriated to religious worfhip in Wales, and the number of Bibles printed at this

this time. The number of parish churches in that country is supposed to be about eight hundred (t). Add to these at random the chapels of ease, and the churches, cathedral and collegiate; and the whole number may amount to nine hundred or a thousand. But I much question whether this publication was numerous enough to supply so many places. The same causes, which procrastinated and delayed the version, might also cramp and lessen the impression; and render it small, scanty, and inadequate even to the publick wants of the country.

IMPRESSIONS of books in general were not at that period so numerous as they are at present, when reading is much more in fashion. I remember to have read somewhere, that Grafton the Printer, when soliciting an exclusive Charter to vend English Bibles, made use of this plea;—That he had,
at

(t) Walker says, 965. Sufferings of clergy, p. 166.

at a great expence, printed a large impreffion of that book, *confifting of fifteen hundred copies.* If fifteen hundred Bibles were reckoned a large number for England; half that number, a quarter of that number, might be thought a very large impreffion for Wales; and if fo, if only five or fix hundred copies were printed off at this time, there might, and, notwithftanding this fupply, there would be a great many chapels and churches in that country yet deftitute of Welfh Bibles. We may imagine that the provifion now made was adequate to the number of places intended to be fupplied; becaufe that feems to be required by law; and becaufe it is right it fhould be fo. But this will not follow, any more than it follows, that the tranflation and impreffion itfelf was finifhed by the 1ft of March, 1566; becaufe it is ordered by Parliament that it fhould be. But however thefe things may have been; let the provifion of this time have been adequate or not;

this

this verſion has ſince received conſiderable alterations.

The tranſlation of the New Teſtament printed in the edition of 1588 had been made, as we have ſeen, by Saleſbury and Davies; and only reviſed and corrected by Morgan. For ſome reaſon or other, Morgan reviſed and corrected it again; and it was ready for the preſs, when he died in 1604 (u). Whether he intended to have the whole Bible reprinted; and in that caſe that was his intention; whether he propoſed only a further ſupply for the churches, or a more general proviſion for the country, is and probably muſt be for ever unknown; and it is likewiſe unknown, whether this corrected verſion of the New Teſtament was ever publiſhed or not. But,

In the reign of James the Firſt, the tranſlation of the New, together with that of the Old Teſtament, underwent the

(u) Ames Typogr. Antiq. p. 435.

the examination and correction of Dr. Richard Parry, Morgan's fucceffor in the See of St. Afaph. The alterations made in confequence of this examination feem to have been confiderable enough to juftify us, fhould we call, what was then publifhed, a new verfion of the Bible into Welfh; as King James, and the perfons employed by him, in the Englifh impreffion of about this time, call their corrections and alterations a new tranflation of the Bible into Englifh.

THIS corrected or new verfion of the Britifh Bible is much the fame with that in ufe at this day. It may be deemed the ftandard tranflation for that language, as King James's Verfion is confidered with regard to the Englifh. It was printed in London by Norton and Bill, printers to his Majefty, in the year 1620. The copy of this impreffion prefented to the King is now in that noble repofitory of antiquities and curiofities, the Britifh Mufeum. *It is a large*

VERSIONS OF THE BIBLE. 29

large handsome folio; it is printed on black letter; it is divided like the former edition; it has large contents of chapters, and the references of King James's Bible in the margin; the sheets of the Old Testament and Apocrypha run E e e e 3; *and the sheets of the New Testament run* Y 2; *it has prefixed to it a calendar and a Latin dedication sacro-sanctæ et individuæ Trinitati, &c. and to King James;* in which the Editor gives us some account of the edition, and of his inducements to undertake it.

HE took considerable liberties, he there tells us, with the former translation; varying and altering it, in such a manner, that it might seem doubtful, whether the version by him now published should be reckoned Parry's, or his predecessors. ' *Quædam,*' says he, ' *cum præcessoris laude retinui; quædam* ' *in Dei nomine mutavi atque sic compegi;* ' *ut et hic sit* αμφιδοξυμενον παραδειγμα, ' *et dictu sit difficile, num vetus an nova,* ' *Morgani an mea, dicenda sit versio.*'

HIS

His inducements or motives for undertaking this publication, he adds in the following remarkable words : ' *Bibliis* ' *in plerifque apud nos Ecclefiis, aut defi-* ' *cientibus aut tritis; et nemine, quantùm* ' *ego audire potui, de excudendis novis* ' *cogitante ; id pro virile conatus fum in* ' *Britannicâ Bibliorum verfione, quod fe-* ' *liciter factum eft in Anglicanâ.*' That is, the former impreffion of the Bible being exhaufted, and *plerifque apud nos Ecclefiis,* many or *moft* of our churches being either without any, or having only worn out and imperfect copies; and nobody, as far as I could learn, *fo much as thinking of a republication;* — in thefe circumftances of this matter, and induced by thefe confiderations, I fet about revifing our tranflation; and, as had been lately done for England, about providing a fupply for the wants of my country, by a new edition of the Britifh Bible, in a better and more correct verfion.

WHEN

WHEN I firſt heard of this edition, printed but a little while after King James had had the Scriptures tranſlated anew into Engliſh, from the original Hebrew and Greek, and publiſhed for a more correct and more perfect Engliſh ſtandard; when I heard of this correction and new edition of the ſame book in the Welſh tongue; I made no doubt but this muſt have proceeded from the care of Government, and had been particularly planned and ordered by his Majeſty. How much muſt I therefore have been ſurpriſed on finding, from what is quoted above, that this was ſo far from being the caſe, *that*, it ſeems, *nobody had ſo much as thought of ſuch a thing*; that Parry was entirely a volunteer in this affair, induced to undertake it merely from the conſideration of the abſolute wants and neceſſities of his country. *Many*, if not *moſt*, of the churches were without Bibles; and we may reſt aſſured there were none elſewhere. Yet no proviſion

is

is made, or likely to be made for their supply, but for the voluntary, but for the spontaneous undertaking of this truly Proteſtant and very Venerable Biſhop.

Dr. John Davies, the learned author of Dictionarium Latino-Britannicum, was Chaplain to the above Biſhop. In 1621, the year after the date of Parry's Bible, Davies publiſhed in Latin his Grammar for the Britiſh tongue. He dedicated his book to the Biſhop his patron. In the preface to that book he tells us, that for above thirty years he had ſpent much of his time in ſtudying the language of his own country, and had ſome concern in both the verſions of the Bible into it. ‘ *Utrique*
‘ *S. S. Bibliorum Interpreti Brit. indig-*
‘ *nus fui adminiſter.*’ Thus modeſtly doth he ſpeak of himſelf. Others ſpeak of him in a different ſtrain : ‘ *In*
‘ *Bibliorum (Britan. ſcilicèt) ultimâ et*
‘ *emendatâ editione, Joannes Davies* peru-
‘ tilem *impendit operam,*’ ſays a Chancellor

VERSIONS OF THE BIBLE. 33

cellor of St. Afaph and Bangor, few years after this time (v).

He was therefore affifting to both our principal Biblical tranflators. He had a confiderable fhare in the fecond verfion and edition of the Welfh Bible, and ought not to be omitted *in an attempt to refcue from oblivion and darknefs the memory and names of the perfons concerned in it*. He feems to have been eminently fitted for fuch a work. He was a thorough mafter of the Britifh tongue. 'He was efteemed, fays Wood, well verfed in the hiftory and antiquities of his own nation, well verfed in the Greek and Hebrew languages, a moft exact critick, an indefatigable perfon, and well acquainted with curious and rare authors (w).'

ALL fubfequent impreffions have, in general, accorded with this edition of
D   1620.

(v) Dict. Lat. Brit. inter Encom. Marg.
(w) Athen. Oxon. vol. 1. p. 597.

1620. There may be some small variations, but they are not material: they affect the size, the letter, or the paper (tho' here we have very little variety) they affect the spelling, or the change in the initials of words, which in this language is remarkable; they respect supplementary words, or the printing in capitals such words as answer to Jehovah, to Lord, to God, &c. printed in capitals in English; or they respect readings and references in the margin, or the division of chapters into paragraphs. Some editions have the year of the world printed at the top, or the side of the page; some add maps, chronological tables, and tables of coins, weights and measures, Hebrew, Greek and Roman;—to adapt the book to the Liturgy, some mark the psalms for the day of the month, and for morning and evening service; and likewise the chapters appointed for morning and evening lessons, throughout the Old Testament. In these and such like instances

VERSIONS OF THE BIBLE. 35

ſtances there may be ſome variations; but in other reſpects, and in general, all impreſſions ſince have been only tranſcripts, or copies, of the verſion and edition of 1620.

There has been but one more folio impreſſion of this book. It came out in 1690, ſeventy years after this time. It was printed at Oxford, not like the former on black letter, but on a common, or good Roman character; otherwiſe it is ſo ſimilar as not to need a particular deſcription. This is ſometimes called Biſhop Lloyd's Bible; and it is ſuppoſed that he had ſome concern in it's publication. He is, I find, the author of the chronology, and of many of the references, printed in moſt of our Engliſh Bibles, particularly the Quarto ones (x). This chronology and theſe references are added, I am told, to this edition of the Welſh Bible. What elſe it has of the learned Biſhop's,

(x) Biogr. Brit. Lloyd, F.

I cannot find. The conduct of the impreffion, if my information is right, was intrufted with Mr. Pierce Lewis, an Anglefey gentleman, then at Jefus College, who it is faid has difcharged his truft accurately and well (y).

THE quantity of books in any of thefe folio impreffions is not known. They were principally, if not folely, intended for publick worfhip; and, for various reafons, I fhould imagine the number of copies printed never much exceeded, if it equalled, the number of churches. But I fhall difmifs, perhaps full late, this part of my fubject, and proceed to give fome account of the octavo editions of the fame book.

FOR upwards of *feventy years*, from the fettlement of the Reformation by Q. Elizabeth; for near *one hundred years*, from Britain's feparation from the Church

(y) MS. Account, penes R. Morris, of the Navy Office, Efq.

Church of Rome, there were *no Bibles* in Wales, but only *in the cathedrals or in the parifh churches and chapels.* There was no provifion made for the country, or for the people in general; as if they had nothing to do with the word of God, at leaft no farther than they might hear it, in their attendance on publick worfhip, once in the week. This is aftonifhing!

THE Bible itfelf may be reckoned a much more ufeful book in the fmaller than in the larger fize. In folio it is expenfive, it is bulky, it is heavy and unmanageable, and not very convenient even for churches. A quarto would be much more handy for this purpofe; that is the fize generally ufed in the churches in Holland; if I miftake not, that is the fize moft commonly ufed in the Englifh cathedrals, and in the Royal and many other chapels. In the fmaller fize it is moft read, and comes into moft hands. It is beft adapted to the ufe of individuals, of fchools, of families, and of many places, appropriated for publick worſhip. I ſuppoſe there may be twenty times the number printed in octavo and under, to what there is printed in folio. Bibles, in octavo and under, become portable and convenient for the pocket, and they become at the ſame time cheaper and more reaſonable.

THE honour of providing for the firſt time a ſupply of this kind for the inhabitants of Wales is due to one or more citizens of London; who, from a generous and noble concern for the good of their fellow-ſubjects, procured at their own expence an octavo impreſſion of the Welſh Bible in 1630, in the reign of Charles the Firſt.

IT gives me particular pleaſure that I can mention ſome of theſe perſons by name; I do it with gratitude and great veneration for their memory; and I could wiſh the names of all concerned might be recorded with honour, and had in everlaſting remembrance. It was a noble

noble inftance of generofity and publick fpirit; tho' it is neither the firft nor the only inftance, wherein citizens of London have taken the lead, and fet others an example, worthy the imitation of the greateft perfonages. Should the reader have an opportunity, let him run over the thirtieth chapter of Stow's Survey of London, and fee there the noble acts of it's citizens. If that lift were continued to the prefent time, I might defy the world to produce it's equal, or any thing near it.

THE indefatigable Mr. Strype tells us (z), that Mr. Rowland Heylin, an Alderman of London, fprung from Wales, *charitably* and *nobly*, at his own coft and charges, in the beginning of the reign of Charles the Firft, caufed the Welfh Bible to be printed in a more portable bulk, being only printed in a large volume before, for the ufe of churches. The firft edition in a portable

(z) Survey of Lond. vol. 2. b. 5. p. 142. edit. 1720.

able fize is the edition of 1630, and muft therefore be the edition referred to by Mr. Strype, and underftood by him to have been printed at the fole charge and expence of that worthy Alderman. Mr. Strype was miftaken in afcribing this matter wholly to Mr. Heylin. Sir Thomas Middleton, a native of Wales, a Magiftrate alfo, and Alderman of London, was a coadjutor, and a generous contributor to this good defign. To thefe two Aldermen, the late Rev. Mr. Griffith Jones joins other citizens of London, whofe names he wifhes to have had, but had not, in his power to mention (a). To the joint and united benevolence and liberality of thefe gentlemen, Wales is indebted for the firft impreffion of the Bible, in a portable bulk and of a fmall price.

In the year 1654, there was a fecond edition of this Bible in octavo, confifting

(a) Welfh Piety for 1742.

fifting of fix thoufand copies. This is the firft account we have met with of the number of copies contained in any impreffion. For this we are indebted to Mr. Charles Edwards, author of a Welfh book, called *Hanes y Ffydd*, written in the laft century, feveral times printed, the firft time with an Oxford *Imprimatur*, Auguft 1, 1676. Edwards doth not inform us to whom we are particularly obliged for this very confiderable fupply, as it muft be then deemed. And for want of particular benefactors to whom we might refer it, I have fometimes been difpofed to amufe myfelf with afcribing it to the temper of the nation, and of the times in which it was granted.

This Bible was publifhed in the year 1654, the firft year of the protectorate of Oliver Cromwell, whofe anceftors are faid to have come from Wales, and whofe family name is faid to have been originally Williams. At this period the caft of the times, the difpofition of the people,

people, of the people in power, and of the people in general, was religious. Attachment to fcripture was the general profeffion. Scripture knowledge was in vogue; and fcripture language, the language in faíhion. Scripture phrafes are taken up and applied to every occafion and event. *The Lord of Hofts—God with us*—&c. were the mottos of the times, the word of battle, the cry of armies, and the ftile of coins, medals, and infcriptions. Thefe very times produced the *London Polyglott Bible*. This temper and genius of the people produced *an Act for the Propagation of the Gofpel in Wales*; and feveral regulations refpecting religion. No wonder then, it fhould alfo produce the publication of the *Welſh* Bible, as proper and neceffary to enforce and eftablifh their own act and regulations.

In a little time this impreffion was exhaufted; and Bibles became fcarce and dear. Upon inquiry in 1674, not above twenty

VERSIONS OF THE BIBLE. 43

twenty copies could be found on fale in the city of London; and not above thirty-two to be purchafed throughout England and Wales. This occafioned another octavo edition, which came out in 1678, and confifted of eight thoufand copies, by much the moft numerous impreffion yet publifhed; one thoufand of which were immediately given away among the poor; and the reft were referved and difpofed in proper places, to be fold at four fhillings per Bible bound.

THE account of this impreffion, of the number of books it contained, and of the manner of difpofing them, is better known, and probably will continue to be more generally known, than the ftate of any other edition of the fame book. This is owing to the merited reputation and fame of Archbifhop Tillotfon; among whofe works there is *a fermon on the death of Mr. Thomas Gouge*, who had a principal hand in this publication of the Britifh Bible.

MR.

Mr. Gouge was a moſt benevolent and generous man. Out of an annual income of one hundred and fifty pounds, he uſed to give away one hundred a year in charity. He made Wales in a particular manner the object of his charitable regards. When between ſixty and ſeventy years of age, he uſed to travel into that country, and with his own hands diſtribute his bounty among the poor and indigent inhabitants. He ſet up among them *a great number of ſchools* (it is ſaid between three and four hundred) to teach people to read Welſh and Engliſh; and he ſupported and continued theſe ſchools for ſeveral years. To render theſe ſchools the more uſeful, he took care to ſupply the people with Welſh books. When he could meet with none fit, in their own language; he cauſed ſuch to be tranſlated from the Engliſh, and printed for their uſe. *The Whole Duty of Man*, *the Practice of Piety*, and ſome other practical Engliſh books are mentioned as tranſlated, and printed by by or for him, with this view. And books of religion, devotion, &c. in the Welsh language, which were not to be had, or very dear; these he caused to be reprinted, particularly the *Book of Common-Prayer*, *the New Testament*, *and the above edition of the Welsh Bible* (b).

It is not to be supposed, that he did all this, at his own cost and charge. Ten times his fortune would not have been sufficient to defray such an expence. The support of so many *schools*, of so many *publications* and *distributions*, must have been the work of a number of persons, who, excited to this charity by his arguments, and more by his example, might employ him to manage and dispose of their joint contributions. Dr. Calamy has preserved a paper, containing an account of his faithful discharge of this trust, audited or attested by Tillotson, Whichcot, Stillingfleet, Pool, &c. (c). BESIDES

(b) Tillotson on Death of Gouge; and Calamy's Account of Ejected Ministers, vol. 2. p. 8.
(c) Calamy ubi supra.

BESIDES thefe gentlemen, eminent for their ftation, learning, or goodnefs, there was another perfon not included in the above lift, yet very active in promoting thefe charitable defigns, for the advantage of Wales; I mean Mr. Stephen Hughes of Swanfey, Glamorganfhire. He feems to have done in the country, what Mr. Gouge did in London. He procured fubfcriptions and donations for this purpofe, and contributed liberally himfelf. He tranflated feveral Englifh books into Welfh. He publifhed, it is faid, near twenty Welfh books, feveral of them at his own expence. Among the reft he collected together and printed the excellent *poems* of the Rev. Mr. Rhŷs Prichard of Llandovery;—a book the moft known, and the moft read, of any in Wales; the Bible alone perhaps excepted. The preceding edition (Cromwell's Bible, if I may fo call it) had been printed very incorrectly. Whole words, and parts of fentences had been
omitted

omitted (d). To rectify thefe miftakes, and to prevent others on the prefent publication, Mr. Hughes took upon him the care of the prefs; and as he was a man of learning, and thoroughly acquainted with the Britifh tongue, this edition was well printed, and came out very correct (e).

These pious and vigorous endeavours of Gouge, Hughes, and others, muft have had a confiderable effect on that country. The fchools, fet up and continued in various parts of it, and the books tranflated and publifhed for the ufe of it's inhabitants, muft have fpread knowledge amongft them, and given them a tafte for reading. The confequence of which was, this numerous impreffion of the Bible was in few years exhaufted, and the book became again fcarce and dear. Mr. Gouge died 1681,

two

(d) Hughes's Preface to Llyfr-Ficar.
(e) Calamy's Account of Ejected Minifters, vol. 2. p. 718.

two or three years after the above edition came out, and confequently before any want of another could be fenfibly felt; but Mr. Hughes lived long enough to difcover it, and to exert himfelf a fecond time in this affair. He fet on foot another impreffion, but did not live to fee it finifhed. He died about the year 1687; but the next octavo edition of this Bible was not publifhed till 1690.

This impreffion was more numerous than any of the preceding. I cannot find the exact number of copies, which it contained; but we are told by Calamy (f), that about ten thoufand were diftributed in Wales by the editor Mr. David Jones, who, it is faid, took a great deal of pains in printing and fpreading Welfh Bibles. It feems that the principal patron of this publication was a noble Lord of the Wharton family; I fuppofe Thomas Baron Wharton, afterward

(f) Calamy's Account of Ejected Minifters, vol. 2d. p. 720.

afterward Viscount Winchendon, Earl and Marquis of Wharton; a zealous Protestant and promoter of the Revolution; a faithful servant to King William; and one of Queen Anne's ministers in the *glorious* part of her reign. Jones was patronized in this undertaking by other persons of quality, besides Lord Wharton; and generously assisted by some ministers and citizens of London (g).

The edition of 1690 *was the last in the seventeenth century. It made the fourth impression in an octavo size; and the seventh in all of this book, before that period. It is not so handsomely printed; not on so good paper, nor with so neat a character as the preceding; otherwise for size, for type, and for number of sheets, they are much alike among themselves, and like to several English impressions of the Bible of about the same date; they are printed pretty close, and the letter is rather small, and therefore*

(g) Ibid. vol. 2. p. 720.

therefore not quite so well for the eye; but yet the book is so portable, so convenient in many respects, that I have often wished we had the same book again printed in this form, both in Welsh and English.

If we attend this subject into the present century, we shall find the state of it altered much for the better. Millions sterling have been expended on works of benevolence, in this country, since the year 1700. Should any one question this, and think the prodigious sum too enormous, let him reflect on the number of hospitals, established in town and country; let him make an estimate at random of the expence of erecting and supporting these hospitals; let him add to these our schools of charity, for the instruction and support of the children of the poor and destitute; to these still add our numerous companies and charitable institutions (some of which distribute annually thousands

VERSIONS OF THE BIBLE. 51

fands of pounds) and befides thefe, the private diftributions of individuals; and when all this is confidered, the above affertion of millions being expended in charity, fince the commencement of the prefent century (though the fum muft feem vaft and prodigious) will not be thought to exaggerate.

To furnifh with Bibles a nation of Proteftants; a nation in the neighbourhood of London and part of Britain; a nation confifting, it may be, of fixty thoufand families, or of no lefs than three hundred thoufand individuals; to furnifh fo many perfons with Bibles, is a defign fo excellent and fo noble, that it cannot but have met with attention and regard, in this age of benevolence, in this exuberance of charity.

WITHIN thefe fifty years laft paft, there have been four impreffions of this book. *The firft was publifhed in* 1718; *the fecond in* 1727; *the next in* 1746; *and the laft in* 1752. *They are all in octavo. The fecond is rather fmaller than* the others. *It is likewise without contents of chapters, and without marginal references;* and for that reason it was never so much valued by the people for whom it was published; such is their attachment, such is their prejudice, to these contents and references; with which, except in this single instance, they have hitherto ever been gratified. *The three other editions are large handsome octavos, on good paper and letter. They have the Apocrypha, contents, and references. They have the year of the world on the top of the page; the church lessons marked in the Old Testament; and the Psalms for morning and evening service, for every day in the month. They have also annexed a scripture index or chronology* (h); *tables of weights and measures; the Psalms in metre; and some hymns, and forms of prayer* (i).

THE

(h) *This index is an epitome of Archbishop Usher's Chronology by Bishop Lloyd. It is taken from the English impression of the folio Bible of* 1701, *and was translated by S. Williams.* MS. Account, penes Mr. Morris, compared with Lewis's Engl. Transl. p. 350.
(i) The Edit. of 1752 had no Apocrypha.

The Bible of the impreſſion of 1718 is commonly called Moſes Williams's Bible, from the Rev. Mr. Moſes Williams, curator of the preſs to that edition. He was vicar of Dyfynog, in the county of Brecon; a gentleman of good literature, who well underſtood the Britiſh and the learned languages. He tranſlated ſeveral books into Welſh. He aſſiſted Dr. Wotton in publiſhing the *Leges Wallicæ*. He gave at the end of his Bible a gloſſary, or interpretation of Hebrew and Greek names; and his impreſſion is reckoned correct and well done.

The Bible of either of the two laſt impreſſions may, for a like reaſon, be called Mr. Morris's Bible (k), from the name of the gentleman who was curator of the preſs to both; a gentleman well verſed in the language and hiſtory of his country; the moſt critically acquainted of any, within my knowledge, with

(k) Supra, p. 35.

with the fubject of thefe papers; as communicative as he is knowing; to whom the author, to whom the reader is obliged for many particulars contained in this account. The edition of 1746 was printed at Cambridge, and has feveral literal errata, occafioned by the curator's living in London, at a diftance from the prefs. The edition of 1752 was more under the curator's infpection, being printed in London (as were all the other editions of this book, except the above and the folio of 1690) and it is, I believe, as correct as any edition whatever of this book.

If I am not miftaken, Wales is more or lefs indebted to the Society for promoting Chriftian Knowledge, for every impreffion within this century. They were the principal promoters of the edition of 1718. Others were admitted to fubfcribe, and at a certain price had any number of books, in proportion to their fubfcriptions. This appears

from

from the propofals for the impreffion, thrown out by the Society in 1714 (l); and feems very fair and likely to take. But what number of copies were printed at this time doth not appear. With regard to the edition of 1727 I have no particular intelligence. I afcribe it to the Society, as the moft likely perfons I can think of, to have been it's patrons and promoters. The two other impreffions are well known to have been undertaken and executed at their expence. They confifted of *thirty thoufand Bibles*, and ftood the Society in *fix thoufand pounds*; which large expence it was enabled to bear, through the generous contributions of multitudes of individuals in town and country. The book was diftributed in Wales, moftly by the Society's members or correfpondents; and ordered to be fold at Four Shillings and Six-pence per Bible, bound. And for this large and liberal fupply, that Society

(l) MS. Account penes Mr. Morris.

Society deserve the grateful acknowledgement of every Briton; and they are hereby desired particularly to accept the thankful acknowledgement of One, with the warmest gratitude, and the highest sense of national obligation.

BESIDES these several editions and versions of this book taken together, there have been other translations, or impressions, of some parts of it, separately published.

A metrical version of the Psalms by Captain Middleton. London printed in 1603, by Thomas Salesbury (m). The book is in the possession of Mr. Morris.

In 1647, the New Testament was printed alone in 12mo, without contents of chapters, or marginal references (n).

In the year following were printed Mr. Archdeacon Pryse's Psalms in metre of the same size (o). I suppose these Psalms must

(m) Ames' Typogr. Antiq. p. 435.
(n) MS. Account, penes Mr. Morris.
(o) Ibid.

muſt have been printed before; but of this I have no account.

The New Teſtament was printed ſeparately in 1654, of a larger character than the Bible of the ſame date (p).

The ſame Teſtament was publiſhed together with the Pſalms, in proſe and metre, by means of Mr. Gouge, &c. in 1672 (q).

The ſame Part was again ſeparately printed in 1752, by means of the Society for promoting Chriſtian Knowledge. And I believe it has been frequently publiſhed by itſelf at Shrewſbury; and may be had, I imagine, at any time.

HAVING thus attended this ſubject to the preſent time, and given the beſt hiſtorical deduction of it, in my power; I ſhall beg leave to hazard ſome few reflections upon it, and ſubmit them to the judgement and candid conſideration of the publick.

I

(p) Teſte Charles Edwards.
(q) MS. Account penes Mr. Morris, &c.

I begin with obferving, that the Britifh verfion of the Bible done in the manner, and under fuch circumftances as have been mentioned, does great honour to the perfons who undertook and effected it. It does honour to their piety and patriotifm. It does honour likewife to their literary abilities, and to the knowledge of the times.

Our tranflators were men of real learning and knowledge. Salefbury, we have feen, was a perfon of liberal education. He feems to have been a good linguift for the age in which he lived; and his tranflation was made directly from the Greek, collated with the Latin. Bifhop Davies was employed in tranflating, from the Hebrew into Englifh, part of the Old Teftament, for what is called Parker's or the Bifhop's Bible (r). Parry, Wood tells us, was on account of his learning promoted by King James to the See of St. Afaph (s). Dean Goodman,

(r) Burnet, Lewis, &c.
(s) Athen. Oxon. vol. 1. p. 727.

Goodman, Dr. Powel, Dr. John Davies, and others, affiftants in this bufinefs, are known to have been men of good literature, and general knowledge. And I conclude from various confiderations, that Dr. Morgan was a perfon of found learning, and well acquainted with the original languages of the Old and New Teftament.

He was a Cantabrigian. But Cambridge has had *no Wood*, *no Athenæ Cantabrigienfes*; for want of which we are often at a lofs for little anecdotes relating to fuch as are brought up at that univerfity. Here however Morgan had his education; and here he received the teftimonials ufually given, in thefe feats of learning, to capacity and improvement. After this, we hear nothing of him till he is encouraged, at his living, fome hundreds of miles from the Capital, as a proper perfon to undertake the tranflation of the Bible, efpecially of the Old Teftament, into the Britifh tongue. His encouragers and approvers

provers are an Archbiſhop, two Biſhops, and others, perſons of learning themſelves, and proper judges of learning and merit of this kind in others. And when he had completed his verſion, Queen Elizabeth gave him a Biſhoprick, as the due reward of his labour. Theſe are ſtrong preſumptions of his being equal to the work he undertook. Beſides, there are, I think, internal proofs, in the tranſlation itſelf, of it's being made directly from the original. I cannot read the Firſt Chapter of Geneſis in Hebrew and in Welſh without coming to this concluſion. Every competent judge of this matter may perhaps be ſatisfied hereof, by the turn of one ſentence frequently repeated in that chapter (t). Here the Welſh is more like the original than any modern tranſlation I know.

I ſhould not have taken notice of theſe things, had it not been for an idle ſtory
recorded

(t) Ver. 5, 8, 13, &c.

VERSIONS OF THE BIBLE. 61

recorded in Ames (u); which seems to insinuate, that Morgan translated only from the English. It is grounded on a single word, *Rev.* chap. 5. ver. 8. of the edition of 1588; and not as Ames has it, of the Testament of 1567. Here, instead of *Phialau*, the Welsh for φιαλαι in Greek, or *vials* in English, *Crythau* is used, which signifies *violins*; and this is supposed to have happened through the translator's having only the English before him; and mistaking even that, and taking *vials* for *viols*, and that again for *violins*, and then rendering it *Crythau*. This undoubtedly is a very gross mistake; but whomsoever it may affect, it should not affect Morgan, who did not translate the Revelations, nor the New Testament. Nor does it affect the real translators of that part of Scripture. In the first edition it is printed right. It is *Phialau*, and not *Crythau*; and the introduction of it into the next
impression

(u) Typogr. Antiq. p. 321.

impreffion cannot have proceeded from ignorance; but may have been the effect of extreme careleffnefs, or, which may be more likely, of mere wantonnefs.

AGAIN, I cannot help lamenting the difadvantages of my countrymen in this refpect, for a confiderable time after the Reformation, and in fome meafure even to this day. Their fellow-fubjects in England had great numbers of Bibles, of different prices and bulk, publifhed in the reigns of Elizabeth, of Edward VI. and of Henry VIII. In the next century they had, as I may fay, an infinite quantity, not only of books, but of editions, printed for their ufe. At prefent (befides what is done in Scotland and elfewhere) the prefs is continually going at three different places in England for this end. Their fupplies are as various as they can wifh; they are as regular and as plentiful as the harveft, or their daily bread. But for the fupply of Wales, there was but one

quarto

quarto impreffion of the New Teftament; and one more of the whole Bible in folio (probably neither of them numerous) during the courfe of the fixteenth century. They had no Bible of a portable fize, and of eafy purchafe, for near one hundred years after the Reformation. They had but two folio and four octavo impreffions in all the feventeenth, and till a good way in the eighteenth century. The whole number, contained in thefe feveral impreffions, might amount to about thirty thoufand Bibles; which, if they had come out all together, and were divided among three hundred thoufand inhabitants, would be only one book between half a fcore perfons. But that would be a wrong method of calculation in this cafe. This may be the fum of what came out at different periods, during one hundred and fifty years. Some part of which time, there might not be as many Bibles as parifhes; and perhaps no fingle fupply before this century

century yielded more than at the rate of *ten books,* some of them probably not above *five books,* for a parish.

HAPPILY, the state of things at present is different. There have been four impressions within the space of the last fifty years; two of them very numerous, containing as many as all the editions before 1700. But still there is not the plenty, nor the variety, enjoyed in other parts of the kingdom. There is frequent scarcity and dearth; generally speaking and for years together, there is no Bible to be had, except by accident. The supplies of it, when they come, come by intervals, and at considerable distances; they proceed from the benevolent, the generous efforts of particular persons or societies, which are irregular and uncertain; and which, if they are plentiful, and especially if the books are given away, occasion a glut for the present, and in few years want again.

CONSIDERING

Considering the prevailing charitable difpofition of the times, I cannot prefage any thing very bad in this cafe, for the future. Suppofing this difpofition to continue, no fcarcity or want will long remain unprovided for. But ftill I could wifh to fee this matter fet upon fomewhat a different footing. Inftead of fupplies, be they ever fo large, thrown out at long and uncertain intervals, I could wifh to have fupplies, regular and ftated. I could wifh to have fupplies for the people in general, and not for any denomination or part of them only; fupplies, adequate to the wants, at leaft to the demands, of the country; and fo difpofed, that any perfon may have recourfe to them, and procure any quantity he pleafes, either for himfelf or others. Such is the ftate of this matter in England; fuch I wifh it to be in Wales; but fuch hitherto it has not been.

The printers to the King's moft excellent Majefty have had a fucceffion of patents,

patents, to the exclufion of all others, except the two Univerfities, for printing Bibles, &c. *in the Englifh tongue.* One or two of thefe patents, in a reign of patents and of James the Firft, fay; *or in any other language* (v). Thefe patents, it is faid, convey an exclufive right to print Welfh Bibles. I would fay nothing to the contrary. I only wifh the patentees would be fo good as to take full poffeffion of their right, and put it to fome ufe. Hitherto they do not feem to have done it. In one hundred and fifty, or two hundred years' time, they have printed (at their own rifk and charge) as many Bibles for Wales, as they have printed Hebrew Teftaments for the Jewifh Synagogue; that is, none at all. As to the folio editions, it may not be quite fo plain; but as to the octavos, we know at whofe expence they were printed. Suppofing the

(v) Bafkett *v.* Univerfity of Camb. in Burrow's Reports, vol. 2. and in Burn's Eccles. Law, vol. 1. p. 347.

the patent-makers originally meant to convey this right; if it is not taken up, there may be some danger of incurring a forfeiture; if a non-user should not be incurred already. But I would make no objection to any thing, provided the country be duly supplied. But if it is not supplied; and if it's not being supplied be owing *to any exclusive grant for printing*; there is then ground of complaint; there is a grievance, *a national grievance*, which ought to be redressed.

But it will be said, patents, like pensions, are beneficial things. If they are for the honour, they should be for the profit, of the pensionee or the patentee. No grants made to a meritorious grantee should be to his detriment. And no patent can be supposed to oblige a gentleman to do any thing to his own hurt. Very true. And I imagine the obstruction in this case arises from want of sufficient profit attending it. I do not understand this business of printing.

I will however venture to say, that it seems very strange to me, that this matter should not promote private profit and advantage, as well as publick benefit.

Suppose in two hundred years' time, or since the Reformation, sixty or seventy thousand Welsh Bibles to have been printed; this, tho' little in comparison with the wants of the country, is yet a considerable number, and at the rate of *three or four hundred Bibles per annum*; besides Testaments, and Common Prayer Books. More than this; since the year 1746, no less than thirty thousand of these Bibles have been printed. In the present year of 1768, and some years back, that is, in twenty years' time and under, they are all taken up, and not a book left for sale. Inquiry has been made in London, and not one is to be found; and, I believe, none in the country, except by accident. Now, this is at the rate of *fifteen hundred books per annum*; should the stated demand be only two-thirds, or but one

half

half of that number, even that would be confiderable; and it may be imagined worth any one's while to attempt to fatisfy. Thoufands of Englifh Bibles are given away annually by generous individuals, and by generous Societies; and I cannot help thinking but fome hundreds in the Welfh language would be annually diftributed by focieties or individuals of fuch a difpofition, if they might have them for that purpofe at a moderate price.

But to any provifion whatever of this kind for the inhabitants of Wales, it is objected;— *That it would be the beft way to prevail with them to neglect and forget their mother-tongue; to learn and become well acquainted with the Englifh language; and thus in time to become of one fpeech, and more entirely one people with the reft of their fellow-fubjects.* This feems to be the wifh and defire of many at prefent; and this feems to have been the aim and intention of Government, ever fince the Reformation. For this end, an Act of Parliament, already mentioned, requires English Bibles, and English Common Prayer Books, to be set up and remain in every church and chapel throughout that country. And with this view, have been projected and attempted methods, taken notice of by *the patriotick and spirited Author of Confiderations on the Illegality of preferring Clergymen unacquainted with the Welsh*, &c.

This is a principal point, and it has materially affected this subject from first to last. It has in fact deprived that people of *the administration of justice* in their own tongue. And it was like to have prevented their ever hearing *the laws of God* and *the gospel of Christ*, as well as *the laws of the land*, in their own language. This, it is said, was solemnly debated at a very honourable board in Queen Elizabeth's time. From the issue of this debate, and from Dr. Morgan's dedication, I conclude that her Majesty was on the side of Wales, upon this

this occasion. Her successor here trod in her steps. King James, though he issued out no commands about the Welsh, as he did about the English Bible, yet was graciously pleased to acquiesce in the publication of it. Two Archbishops of Canterbury at least have thought it right that the Welsh should have a Bible. One distinguished patriot and peer of the realm, several bishops, and many private gentlemen are mentioned as patrons and abettors on this side. I have wished, I have tried to find out others on the same side, but can find none. Here history is silent; and I must be silent also.

It will be more agreeable to me, and more to my purpose to remove, if I am able, this capital objection against the publication of the British Bible. For this purpose I shall attempt to shew — *the insignificance of the end* here intended; *the impropriety and inefficacy of the measures*, here proposed *to accomplish this end*, supposing the end to have been ever

ever so important; and that there are other methods, *much more suitable*, and that will be *more effectual*, to answer this end.

WHATEVER veneration I may have for my mother's tongue; for an ancient, expressive, and sonorous language; the original, and once the general language of this country, and perhaps of Europe; I would yet willingly give it up for important, for valuable considerations. The objection proposes the forgetting of the Welsh, and the learning of the English, as something good and beneficial; as *best* for somebody. Let us consider therefore the advantages attending it, and who are like to receive the benefit.

THESE advantages cannot extend to all the numerous subjects of his most gracious Majesty King George, throughout the several parts of his extensive dominions. This is of no more consequence to the generality of them, than to the dwellers in Mesopotamia, or in Patagonia.

VERSIONS OF THE BIBLE. 73

Patagonia. Not to fpeak of our American colonifts (who I dare fay care very little what language is ufed among the mountains of Wales) not to fay any thing of our fellow-fubjects at a great diftance;—what doth it fignify to a perfon refiding in Scotland, in Yorkfhire, in London, or even in Briftol; whether the inhabitants of Yfgyryd Fawr, or of Penmaen Mawr, talk Welfh or any other language to their own families or neighbours? whether they pray to God, read his word, or tranfact their civil affairs in their own, or in the Englifh tongue? If they could talk twenty languages, or do their bufinefs without any language, it is nothing to thofe who have no connection, or correfpondence with them. To fuch as have occafion to go into that country, whether North or South Britons;—to itinerants in law, in phyfick, or divinity; to itinerants for bufinefs, for curiofity, for fome purpofe, or to no purpofe, it may be of ~~fome~~ confequence. It might be well, it would

be

be convenient for them, if his Majefty's good fubjects in Wales were all Englifh; but however it can hardly be defired, that a whole nation fhould forget their own tongue, and learn another for them; and the only reafonable and eafy method for removing this inconvenience would be for fuch perfons, before they go to that country, to take care to learn Welfh.

If this is of little or no confequence to his Majefty's fubjects refiding in England, Scotland, &c; let us confider what may be the confequence with regard to fuch of thefe as are refiding in Wales; the people here particularly interefted. Here again, I own, it feems to me of very little moment; I mean, to thefe who are refidents, or ftay at home; who in every country muft be by far the majority. The general, the common bufinefs and concerns of civil, of religious, and focial life may be tranfacted, I fuppofe, as well in Welfh as in Englifh. A Cambro Briton may mind his farm and his merchandize, if he has any;

any; he may fow his corn, and bring home his harveſt; he may live as long, and do as much good, with only his own mother-tongue, as if he had twenty tongues befides. But as to thofe who are non-refidents, who leave their native country, and come over to England; as to thofe who crofs the Severn, the Wye, or the Dee; thofe who come up to London, and have a mind to dif-tinguifh themfelves in the metropolis;— to them the Welfh or another language is ar. indifferent. The Englifh is of advantage, is neceffary; and it is their perfonal concern to learn and attain it.

This matter, in this way of confidering it, cannot appear of any great confequence. It is a mere *affair of convenience*, of convenience comparatively to few, to one in a hundred, to three thoufand, may be, out of three hundred thoufand inhabitants, to whom in general it is of little importance. It might be convenient, if all the world was now, as it was in the days of Noah, of one

fpeech

speech and of one language. This might facilitate travelling; it might promote trade and correspondence among the different countries and nations of the earth; but for all that, I never heard of any law made, nor of any bill brought into any Senate, for extirpating tongues in general, and establishing some one common and universal language. If a formal decree may have been proper for the purpose of extirpating the Welsh tongue; why not another equally formal and weighty to abolish all dialects of the English but one? to put an end to Irish inaccuracies and blunders? and to give a pure pronounciation and a sweet accent to the inhabitants of Edinburgh, of Northumberland or Devonshire? Again,

IF we grant *the end* here to be worthy, and of greater importance than it seems to be; *the methods* made use of to accomplish this end, will yet remain very improper and disproportioned. To bring about

about an *uniformity of language* between two neighbouring nations, fubjects of the fame fovereign, in a ftate of perfect harmony and peace;—what muft be done? Why, *The Holy Bible* muft be withholden from one of them; *the word of God* muft be withdrawn from one people, till they can all underftand it in another tongue; that is, it muft be for ever withholden from thoufands who never can, nor will, learn any other. To defcribe here, is to expofe. The very naming of thefe means muft furely be fufficient to fhow them to be, to the laft degree, improper and prepofterous. They affect the religion of a people; they infringe the rights of confcience; they interfere with their duty to God, the care of their fouls, and their eternal falvation; with which no fchemes of human policy fhould interfere, *on any account*, much lefs on account of a mere trifling inconvenience.

HERE lies the great, the unanfwerable objection to thefe meafures, for a change
of

of language. They affect, they deprive a man of what he confiders as effential to his moft important interefts, for a trifle, for nothing to him. He is born in a certain country, he learns the language of his parents and of his country, as naturally and as innocently, as he fucks his mother's breafts, or breathes the common air. He has neither opportunity nor ability to learn any other tongue. And what is the confequence? He muft never hear of a Saviour or falvation;— not becaufe the gofpel was never heard in the land, nor becaufe he is under an Anti-chriftian government. No; his fuperiours are Chriftians, are Proteftants; the Gofpel is in his neighbourhood; and may be preached in his language as well as in any other;—but it muft not be read nor preached in it; *becaufe*, fhould it be, it will obftruct *the spread and progrefs of another language.* Thus difproportioned are the means to the end. They appear highly abfurd and

and preposterous, when considered only in their aspect or relation one to another.

They appear still worse, if considered as coming from a Christian magistracy or government. They are diametrically opposite to the genius and spirit of Christianity. The wise, the divine author of that scheme of grace and mercy conferred upon his ministers the gift of tongues, the power of conveying their doctrines and instructions in every language, that they might speedily spread his religion among the Heathens. Perfectly needless such a measure, say the wiser abettors of this scheme. Let people forget their original language; let them endeavour to learn and become acquainted with another; and then, if they live long enough, let them be instructed in the principles and duties of Christianity. This is the genuine voice and language of such a conduct; and I know no way of excusing or palliating these measures, except upon the principles of Heathenism or Popery. If the design was to abolish
Christianity,

Chriftianity, and to introduce the Pagan religion; then let the Bible be taken away from the people. Or, if the defign was to extirpate the Proteftant religion, and to promote the eftablifhment and growth of Popery; then let the light of the fcriptures be put out; and let the word of God be had only in a language not underftood. This, in a Papift, may be the more readily excufed and tolerated, as it is perfectly in character. He is engaged in an oppofition, he avows an oppofition to fcripture; and would withhold it not only from *one*, but from *every* nation. He is confiftent, he is uniform and impartial, in his enmity to this light of the word; and in his attachment to darknefs and ignorance. But in a Proteftant this is inexcufable. It is not to be tolerated. It is contrary to his profeffion and principles. For him, to withhold the Bible from *a part* of a kingdom, or of a people, is not only a little pitiful partiality; but quite inconfiftent with his religion and character.

AFTER

After all, thefe difproportioned and prepofterous, thefe *unproteftant* and *unchriftian* methods, tho' purfued with rigour and feverity, will not *enfure the end propofed*. Suppofe neither the name nor the religion of Chrift to be known or heard of, in the principality of Wales; yet the language of it might fubfift, and I believe would fubfift, in fpite of every effort of this nature to deftroy it. Violent meafures hardly ever anfwer the expectation. In general, they foon fpend themfelves, and end in nothing. They may do mifchief; they may diftrefs a perfon or a party; they may fhow the difpofition and temper of the times; or they may gratify the rage of a perfecuting tyrant; and but very little more. The thing principally aimed at, is yet unaccomplifhed, perhaps retarded, and not forwarded. Witnefs the heathenifh perfecutions of the Apoftles and primitive difciples of Chrift. Witnefs Chriftian perfecutions of Heathens, of Jews, and of one another. Witnefs Popifh perfecutions

cutions of Proteſtants; and Proteſtant perſecutions of their own members and of Papiſts. I do not mean to inſinuate that any ſuch violence and ſeverity has been practiſed in the preſent caſe. I only ſay, that ſuppoſe they had been practiſed, they would very probably have proved fruitleſs and ineffectual.

BRITONS in Wales, without the Bible, preſerved their language and diſtinction for hundreds of years, preceding the Reformation. The inhabitants of the Iſle of Man have *never* had a Bible in their mother-tongue; yet they have retained it through many generations down to the preſent time. And now at laſt, in *the eighteenth century* of Chriſtianity, they are like *to begin* to read the ſcripture in their own language. I do not find that there has been above *one* edition of this book ever printed, for the uſe of Scotland and Ireland; yet the Iriſh or Erſe inhabitants of both theſe countries do ſtill retain their original language. They uſe it in common at
this

this day; and abundance of them understand not a word of Englifh. This probably, may I not fay? this certainly, would have been the cafe with the inhabitants of Wales, if they had never been favoured with the word of God. They are the moft confiderable body of ancient Celts on the face of the earth. They are much more numerous than the Manks. They are more confiderable for number, than the Erfe in Scotland, or their brethren in Ireland. They are more collected together, and more diftinct from their neighbours, than either of the two laft mentioned people. And for that very reafon I conclude, that they would have retained their language to this day, though they never had had a Britifh verfion of the Bible.

It will be faid, the Cornifh have wholly forgotten their original tongue, and are become entirely Englifh. I know it; but I will not allow this to be entirely, if at all, owing to the nonexiftence of the Scripture in Cornifh.

Other caufes more fuitable, more efficacious, may be affigned for this event. The inhabitants of Cornwall are not fo numerous as the inhabitants of Wales. They were never fo diftinct and feparate from others, as their brethren on the other fide of the Briftol channel. *No Offa's dyke in that part of Britain. They have never been cooped in by hedges and ditches, or other barriers lefs ruftick indeed, but more difagreeable and hoftile. They were never flaughtered by multitudes for a fong* (w). *They were never punifhed for being Cornifh; never excluded the protection of government; never denied legal redrefs on complaints of injuftice and oppreffion; nor ever difqualified as a people, by Acts of Parliament, from holding places of honour, or of profit, in any part of the kingdom* (x).

THE

(w) Welfh Bards maffacred by Edward I.
(x) Statutes of Henry IV. and Greefs of Prince Llewelyn, &c. in Powel's Hiftory of Wales, p. 346. &c.

The abfence of thefe things, with regard to Cornwall, kept open a free communication with England; and facilitated a coalition and famenefs of language. Commerce, and a reciprocation of benefits, always fubfifted between that county and the counties adjoining; and the Cornifh tongue gradually and infenfibly gave way to the fuperiour genius of the Englifh. Four hundred years ago, it feems to have extended much beyond the prefent limits of the county. In Richard of Cirencefter's map (y), Somerfetfhire was occupied by the *Cimbri*, probably the Cornifh, who are fince retired beyond the Tamar; but fo infenfibly, that hiftory has taken no notice of their retreat. In the laft century they retained fomething of their original tongue; but at prefent it is quite extinct (z); and this feems to have been the natural and fure effects of their friendly intercourfe with their neighbours.

(y) About the year 1340.
(z) Borlafe's Nat. Hift. of Cornwall, p. 316.

But the exiftence of the above reftrictions and hardfhips long prevented the fame effects from taking place, with regard to the principality. While thefe reftraints, &c. continued, they promoted enmity and refentment; they were the occafion of ill blood and ill offices; of endlefs depredations and mifchiefs. They feem to have fubfifted with the greateft rigour and feverity, under the princes of the houfe of Lancafter; probably on account of the attachment of the Welfh to the contrary party. Under the Tudors, they were partly repealed, and it may be totally difufed; but yet they were not entirely abrogated till the year 1623 (a); not a century and a half ago. They ftill fubfift in the ftatute books of this realm; to fhow, we will fuppofe, *how fubjects of England were treated in days of yore.* I would beg leave to recommend the printing of them in future, — not in *black*, but in *red* letters, as more defcriptive

(a) 21 James I. chap. 28.

descriptive of their true character and *Draconick* severity; and the better to distinguish them from the more equal and more gentle laws of *Britannia* to her children.

Though disagreeable, it was necessary, to take notice of these particulars, in order to come at the real causes of the extinction of the Cornish, and of the preservation of the British tongue. For the reasons above-mentioned, the state of the two languages must be very different at the time of the Reformation. The Cornish had been long on the decline, and was approaching to it's exit; but the Welsh was in full strength and vigour. The people of the former language, as acquainted in general with the English, might do without any version of the Scripture for their use. The other people wanted it, and had it; but, notwithstanding that, their language has ever since been on the decline. And so little has the Bible affected this matter, that the language has declined the moſt, when there has been the greateſt quantity of Welſh Bibles. Since the commencement of this century, the Welſh tongue has loſt, and the Engliſh hath gained ground, more than in any other period of the ſame duration. The cauſes of this decay of the one, and of the progreſs of the other, are, in my view of the matter, the preſent good underſtanding and friendſhip, the preſent daily intercourſe and reciprocation of benefits, happily ſubſiſting between the two nations. May this diſpoſition and conduct ever ſubſiſt! May this temper and behaviour ever continue and prevail! though this declining condition of the language ſhould prove *mortal*, and end in it's *death*.

Though I muſt confeſs, when I conſider the preſent ſtate of the trade and intercourſe between theſe two nations, I cannot ſee that England will gain much by the utter extinction of the Britiſh tongue.

From Chepſtow weſtward, round by Milford to Holy-head and Cheſter, Wales is environed by the Briſtol and the Iriſh channel, or the ocean. In all this length of coaſt, not a Welſh veſſel is to be ſeen bound to or from any diſtant part of the globe; and hardly a boat or a coaſter, except for London, Briſtol, or ſome other place in England. Throughout the whole extent of the Principality, hardly a perſon is to be ſeen but has *ſomething*, and many of them have *almoſt every thing Engliſh* about them. The lower and middling ſort of people may be clad in cloth, flannel, &c. manufactured at home; the inhabitants of the towns, and the gentry in the country, may eat their own bread and mutton, and drink their own home-brewed ale; but in general they are clothed after the Engliſh faſhion, and in the manufactures of England. Hence *moſt* of the goods in *every* ſhop in that country. Hence the *principal* of their clothing, of their furniture, and of their beverage, &c.

&c. Hence *many* of the articles of common life, and *all* the articles of luxury. I would fain know, *what* England would have more? What more *could* it have, if every individual in that country fpake nothing but Englifh? What more *can* it's trading cities and towns expect from any part of the king's dominions?

Ireland and Scotland wear much of their own manufactures, and provide confiderably for others. Scarce a county or confiderable village in England but is noted for fome particular manufacture and article of commerce. But Wales manufactures next to nothing; it's iron, it's moft confiderable article, it works little further than to make horfe-fhoes and plow-fhares. What is wifhed to take place and to continue, but wifhed perhaps in vain, with regard to our colonies in America, is actually, is notorioufly the cafe in the Principality. It fends to England for every thing. Whatever reproach this may be to the Welfh, it is no difhonour, at leaft no difad-

vantage

VERSIONS OF THE BIBLE.

vantage to the Englifh; and they know their interefts too well not to fupply every demand readily and plentifully. And Welfh Bibles, confidered as an article of commerce, may have been perhaps the only commodity they ever granted grudgingly or fparingly.

UPON the whole, in whatever view I confider this defign of difcontinuing the language of Wales, and of eftablifhing the Englifh in it's ftead; I cannot think it any way fo important as is pretended. It feems to me to be very immaterial, efpecially to England; and I fhould therefore be a good deal unconcerned about it. But when I confider the meafures, propofed to accomplifh this end, I can no longer be indifferent. I feel, I avow a warmth and emotion; and I think it becomes me. W̶a̶s̶ I an Englifhman or a Scotchman, my feelings here, I apprehend, would be the fame. And I fhould look upon it as a duty, to the utmoft of my power, to

bear

bear a publick teftimony againft meafures, fo prepofterous and ineffectual; againft meafures of fuch pernicious and deftructive confequences; againft meafures, tending — not to anfwer the end propofed, or to make the people of Wales ceafe to be Welfh, and become Englifh, but tending to make them ceafe to be Proteftants; to make them ceafe to be Chriftians; ceafe to be loyal fubjects, and good men.

APPEN-

APPENDIX.

N°. I.

Dedication prefixed to the New Teſtament printed in 1567.

To the moſt vertuous and noble Prince Elizabeth, by the grace of God, of England, Fraunce and Ireland, Queene, Defender of the Faith, &c.

WHEN I call to remembrance, as well the face of the corrupted religion in England, at what tyme Paule's Churcheyarde in the Citie was occupied by makers of alabaſter images to be ſet up in Churches; and they of Paternoſter-rowe earned their lyving by makyng of Pater-noſter bedes only; they of Ave-Lane by ſelling Ave-bedes; of Crede-lane

Crede-lane, by makying Crede-bedes; as alfo the vaine rites crepte into our countrey of Wales, whan, infteade of the lyvyng God, men worfhipped dead images of wood and ftones, belles and bones, with other fuch uncertain reliques I wot not what; and withal confider our late general revolt from Godde's moft holy worde once receaved, and dayly heare of the lyke enforced uppon our brethren in forain countryes, having moft piteoufely fufteined great calamities, bitter afflictions, and merciles perfecutions; under which verye many doe yet ftyll remaine; — I cannot, moft Chriftian Prince, and gracious Soveraine, but even as dyd the poore blynde Bartimeus or Samaritane lepre to our Saviour, fo I com before your Majeftie's feete, and there lying proftrate, not onely for myfelf, but alfo for the delivery of many thoufandes of my countrey folkes from the fpiritual blyndnes of ignoraunce, and fowl infection of olde Idolatrie and falfe fuperftition, moft humbly and dutifully

VERSIONS OF THE BIBLE. 95

fully to acknowlege your incomparable benefite beſtowed upon us in graunting the ſacred Scriptures (the verye remedie and ſalve of our goſtly blyndnes and leproſie) to be had in our beſt knowen tongue; which as far as ever I can gather (thoughe Chriſt's trewe Religion ſometyme flooriſhed emong our Aunceſters the old Britons) yet were never ſo entierlye and univerſallye had, as we now (God be thanked) have them.

Our countreymen in tymes paſſed were indede moſt loth (and that not wythout goud cauſe) to receave the Romiſh religion, and yet have they nowe fynce (ſuch is the domage of evyll cuſtome) bene loth to forſake the ſame, and to receave the goſpell of Jeſus Chriſt. But after that thys nation, as it is thought, for their apoſtaſie had ben ſore plagued wyth long warres, and finally vanquiſhed and by rigorouſe lawes kept under; yet at the laſt it pleaſed God of his accuſtomed clemencie to looke down agayne upon them, ſending a moſt godly and noble

David

David and a wyfe Salomon, I meane Henry the feventh and his fonne Henry the eight (both Kynges of moft famous memorie, and your Grace's father and grandfather) who gracioufly releafed their paynes and mitigated their intolerable burthens, the one wyth Charters of Liberties, the other wyth Actes of Parlyament, by abandoning from them al bondage and thraldome, and incorporating them wyth his other loving Subjectes of England.

Thys, no doubt, was no fmall benefit touchyng bodyly welth; but thys benefit of your Majeftie's providence and goodneffe excedeth that other, fo far as the foule doeth the bodye. Certaine noble women (whereof fome were chiefe rulers of thys nowe your Ifle of Britain) are by Antiquitie unto us for their finguler learning and heroical vertues hyghely commended, as Cambra the Fayré, Martia the Good, Bunducia the Wariar, Claudia Rufina mencioned in S. Paule's Epiftle, and Helena, mother of

the

the great and fyrſt Chriſtian Emperour Conſtantinus Magnus, and S. Urſula of Cornwal, with ſuch other, who are alſo at thys day ſtyl renowmed. But of your Majeſtie, I may, as I thynk, right well uſe the wordes of that Kinge, who ſurnamed himſelfe Lemuel: *Many daughters have don vertuouſly; but thou ſurmounteſt them all. Favour is deceiptfull, and beautie is vanitie; but a woman that feareth the Lord, ſhe ſhal be prayſed.* For if M. Magdalen, for the beſtowyng of a boxe of material oynetment, to annoynct Chriſte's carnal body, be ſo famouſe thorowe out all the world where the goſpell is preached;—howe muche more ſhall your munificence, by conferring the unction of the holy Ghoſt, to annoynct his ſpiritual body the Churche, be ever had in memorie?

But to conclude and to drawe neare to offer up my vowe. Wher as I, by our moſt vigilant Paſtours the Biſhopes of Wales, am called and ſubſtituted, though unworthy, ſomewhat to deale in the peruſing and ſetting fourth of

thys

thys fo worthy a matter, I thynk it my moſt bounden duetie here in their name to preſent to your Majeſtie (as the chiefeſt fiyrſt fruict) a booke of the Newe Teſtament of our Lorde Jeſus Chriſt, tranſlated into the Britiſh language, which is our vulgare tongue; wyſhyng and moſt humbly praying, if it ſhall ſo ſeme good to your wyſedome, that it myght remayne in your M. Librarie for a perpetuall monument of your gracioufe bountie ſhewed herein to our countrey, and the Church of Chriſt there. And would to God that your Grace's Subjectes of Wales might alſo have the whole booke of God's woorde brought to like paſſe:—then might their felow ſubjectes of England rejoycingly pronounce of them in theſe wordes, *The people that ſate in darknes have ſeene a great lyght; they that dwelled in the land of the ſhadowe of death, upon them hath the lyght ſhyned. Bleſſed are the people that be ſo, yea bleſſed are the people, whoſe God is the Lord.* Yea, then wold they both together thus brotherly ſay, *Come, and*

and let us go up to the mountaine of the Lord, to the houſe of Jaacob, and he wyll teache us hys wayes, and we wyll walke in hys pathes, &c.

AND thus to end, I beſeeche Almyghtye God, that as your Grace's circumſpect providence doth perfectlye accompliſh and diſcharge your princely vocation and governaunce towardes all your humble ſubjectes, that we alſo on our part may toward God and your highnes demeane ourſelfes in ſuch wyſe, that his juſtice abrydge not theſe halcyons and quiet dayes (which hetherto ſince the begynning of your happie Reigne have moſt calmely and peaceably continued) but that we may long enjoy your gracious preſence, and moſt proſperous Reigne over us; which we beſeeche God, for our Saviour Jeſus Chriſte's ſake moſte mercifullye to graunt us. Amen.

Your M A J E S T I E ' S
Moſt humble and
Faithfull Subject,
William Saleſbury.

N°. II.

Dedication prefixed to the Bible printed in 1588.

Illuftriffimæ, Potentiffimæ, Sereniffimæque Principi ELISABETHÆ, Dei Gratiâ, Angliæ, Galliæ, & Hiberniæ Reginæ, Fidei veræ & Apoftolicæ Propugnat. &c. Gratiam, & Benedictionem in Domino fempiternam.

QUANTUM Deo Optimo Maximo Majeftas veftra debeat, Auguftiffima Princeps (ut opes, potentiam, & admirabilem ingenii ac naturæ dotem taceam) non folùm gratia, quâ apud plurimos pollet rariffimâ; & eruditio, quâ præ cæteris ornatur variâ; & pax, quâ præ vicinis fruitur almâ, ejufque numquàm fatis admiranda protectio,

quâ

quâ & hoſtes nupèr fugavit atroces, & multa ac magna pericula fempèr evaſit feliciſſimè; verùm etiàm cum primis eximia illa pietas, toto orbe celebrata, quâ ipſe V. M. imbuit & ornavit; nec non veræ religionis & propagandæ & propugnandæ ſtudium propenſiſſimum, quo fempèr flagrâſtis, clariſſimè atteſtantur.

NAM (ut & gentes alias, & reliqua præclarè à vobis geſta, jam prætere16am) quàm piam curam veſtrorum Britannorum habuit V. M. hoc unum, quòd Sacroſanɛti Dei Verbi inſtrumenta utraque, vetus ſcilicèt & novum, unà cum illo libro, qui precum publicarum formam, & ſacramentorum adminiſtrandorum rationem præſcribit, in Britannicum fermonem verti non modò benignè permiferit, fed fummorum inclytiſſimi hujus regni comitiorum auɛtoritate follicitè fanxiverit, fempèr conteſtari valet. Quod idem noſtram ignaviam & fegnitiem ſimul prodit; quòd nec tam gravi neceſſitate moveri, nec tam commodâ

lege

lege cogi potuerimus, quin tam diu res tanti (quâ majoris effe momenti nihil unquàm potuerit) intacta penè remanferit. Nam illam Liturgiam, cum Novo Teftamento duntaxat, Reverendus ille Pater Richardus, piæ memoriæ Menevenfis Epifcopus (auxiliante Gulielmo Salefburio, de noftrâ Ecclefiâ optimè merito) annis abhinc viginti Britannicè interpretatus eft

Quâ re quantum noftratibus profuerit, facile dici non poteft. Nam præterquàm quòd vulgus noftrum, quæ Britannicè atque Anglicè fcripta tunc erant, invicem comparantes, Anglici fermonis nuper evaferunt peritiores; ad veritatem tum docendam tum difcendam ifto labore conduxit plurimùm. Tum enim vix unus & alter Britannicè concionari valebant, quòd verba, quibus Britannicè explicanda erant quæ in Scripturis facris facra tractantur myfteria, vel Lethæis quafi aquis deleta prorsùs evanuerant, vel defuetudinis quodam quafi cinere obducta atque fepulta jacuerant;

rant; ut nec docentes quæ vellent fatis apertè explicari, nec audientes quæ explicabantur, fatis felicitèr intelligere valerent. Scripturarum præfereà quæ effent teftimonia, quæve earundem explicationes, Scripturis minùs affueti dijudicare nequibant; adeò ut quùm ad conciones convolarent avidi, & iifdem intereffent feduli, incerti tamèn dubiique difcedebant plerique; — ac fi thefaurum inveniffent amplum, quem effodere non poterant, aut epulis interfuiffent lautis, quibus vefci non daretur.

JAM verò, D. O. M. benignitate eximiâ, veftrâque curâ egregiâ, & Præfulum folicitudine pervigili, hujufque Interpretis labore & induftriâ effectum eft, ut & concionatores longè plures paratiorefque, & auditores magis dociles habeamus. Quæ utraque ut piis funt cordi, ita adhuc eorum voto neutrum vel mediocritèr refpondet. Quum enim prius illud inftrumentum, alterius occultata prædictio, adumbrata figura, &

indubius

indubius teftis noftratibus hactenùs defideretur; Quot (pro dolor) exempla latent! Quot promiffiones delitefcunt! Quot confolationes occultantur! Quot denique monitionibus, exhortationibus, dehortationibus, veritatifque teftimoniis invitus caret populus nofter, quos V. M. regit, curat & amat; quorum æterna falus Satanæ foli, ejufque fatellitibus invifa, hactenùs periclitata eft plurimùm; quum vivat quifque per fidem, fides verò fit ex auditu, auditus etiam per verbum Dei, quod hucufqùe fermone peregrino delitefcens noftratibus parùm infonuit.

Quum igitur reliquarum Scripturarum interpretationem in linguam Britannicam tam utilem, imò tam neceffariam effe viderem (etfi & propriæ imbecillitatis, & ipfius rei magnitudinis, & quorundam ingeniorum κακοφυΐας recordatio me diù deterruerit) piorum precibus acquiefcens, ut hoc opus graviffimum, moleftiffimum, nec non ingratiffimum multis, aggrederer, memet exorari paffus fum. Quod cùm vix aggreffus effem, & rei

difficultate

difficultate, & impensarum magnitudine pressus, in limine (quod aiunt) succubuissem, & solum Pentateuchum ad prelum perduxissem; nisi Reverendissimus in Christo Pater,* Cantuariensis Archiepiscopus, literarum Mæcenas optimus, veritatis propugnator acerrimus, & ordinis ac decori prudentissimus observator (qui, ex quo Britannis, sub vestiâ Majestate, tam prudentissimè tam justissimè præfuit, nostratium tum obedientiam tum acumen animadvertens, animo benigno eos posteà prosecutus est; sicuti & illi ejus laudem sempèr decantant) ut progrederer effecisset, & adjuvisset liberalitate, auctoritate, & consilio. Cujus ad exemplum, alii boni viri opem mihi maximam tulerunt. Quorum hortatu, industriâ, atque labore motus, fultus, & adjutus sæpè; quum non modò vetus instrumentum totum interpretatus sim, sed novum etiam, inemendatâ quadâm scribendi ratione (quâ plurimùm scatebat)

* JOANNES WHITGIFT.

bat) repurgaverim, cui eadem dicare fas atque confentaneum fit, dubius hæfito. Quum vel meæ ipfius indignitatis fummæ recordor, vel V. M., fplendorem eximium intueor, vel ipfius Dei (cujus vices gerit) numen quoddam in eâdem fplendens animadverto; ad tam facrum accedere fulgorem reformido. Contrà verò, rei ipfius dignitas (quæ fuo quafi jure veftram tutelam vendicat) novas mihi vires auget. Deindè, cùm alterum inftrumentum, Britannicè impreffum, tam æquo, benigno, & regio animo fufcipere dignabimini, huic alium venari patronum, & imprudentiæ, & injuriæ, & ingratitudinis effe judico. Sic etiam quæ inter fe tantoperè cohærent atque conveniunt, fejungenda non effe, quin, quæ reverà eâdem funt, eâdem quoque in bibliothecâ, eorum reponantur exemplaria, cenfeo. Quod idem ut Veftra cenfeat M. fupplex rogo & obteftor, necnon fummis precibus contendo, animo benigno conatibus meis ut afpiret; quippè qui veftrarum legum auctoritate nituntur,

VERSIONS OF THE BIBLE.

nituntur, veſtri populi ſaluti inſerviunt, & veſtri Dei gloriam ſpectant; quos etiam veſtri tum pro veritate, tum in Britannos ſtudii, monumentum perpetuum, necnon Britannorum erga V. M. amoris propenſiſſimi teſſeram, fore confido.

Si qui, conſenſûs retinendi gratiâ, noſtrates ut Anglicum ſermonem ediſcant adigendos eſſe potiùs, quàm Scripturas in noſtrum ſermonem vertendas eſſe volunt;—dum unitati ſtudent, ne veritati obſint, cautiores eſſe velim; &, dum concordiam promovent, ne religionem amoveant, magis eſſe ſollicitos opto. Quamvis enim ejuſdem inſulæ incolas, ejuſdem ſermonis & loquelæ eſſe magnoperè optandum ſit; æquè tamèn perpendendum eſt, iſtud ut perficiatur, tantum temporis & negotii peti, ut intereà Dei populum, miſerrimâ illius verbi fame, interire velle aut pati, nimis ſit ſævum atque crudele. Deindè, non dubium eſt, quin religionis quàm ſermonis ad unitatem plùs valeat ſimilitudo

litudo & confenfus. Unitatem præterea pietati, utilitatem religioni, & externam quandam inter homines concordiam eximiæ illi paci, quam Dei verbum humanis animis imprimit præferre, non fatis pium eft. Poftremò, quàm non fapiunt, fi verbi divini in maternâ linguâ habendi prohibitionem, aliena ut edifcatur, quicquam movere opinantur? Religio enim, nifi vulgari linguâ edoceatur, ignota latitabit. Ejus verò rei quam quis ignorat, ufum, dulcedinem & pretium etiam nefcit, nec ejus acquirendæ gratiâ quicquam laboris fubibit. Quamobrèm, roganda eft V. M. ut nullius rationis fpecie impediatur (nec impedietur fat fcio) quin quos cæpit beare beneficiis, augere velit; quos uno inftrumento ditavit, altero dignetur; quibus unum veritatis uber præbuit, alterum concedat; & quod efficere ftuduit, perficere conetur: nempè ut omnis vefter populus mirabilia Dei fuo fermone audiat, & omnis lingua laudet Deum.

Cœleftis

Cœleftis ille Pater, qui imbecillitatem humanam, fœmineum fexum, & virgineam indolem, tam heroicis virtutibus in V. M. ornâffe dignofcitur, ut & miferis folamen & hoftibus terror, & mundi Phœnix eadem hactenùs extiterit, propitius concedat; cælefti fpiritu ita regatur, divinis donis adornetur, & alis Altiffimi protegatur/impofterum, ut longæva mater in Ifrael, pia Ecclefiæ nutrix, & ab hoftibus femper tuta, vitiorum hoftis eadem permaneat; ad D. O. M. sempiternam gloriam, cui omne imperium, honos, & laus in omne ævum. Amen.

Sereniffimæ Veftræ Majeftati,

Omni Reverentiâ,

Subditiffimus

Gulielmus Morgan.

Nomina

Nomina eorum, qui præ cæteris * *hoc opus promovere conati funt.*

Reverendi Patres, Afaphensis & Bangorensis Epifcopi, libros, quos petii, mutuò concefsêre, & iftud opus examinare, perpendere atque approbare dignati funt.

GABRIEL GOODMAN, Weftmonafterienfis Decanus, Vir re & nomine valdè bonus, omnique pietati deditiffimus, quæ interpretatus fueram relegenti ita mihi adfuit affiduus, ut & labore & confilio me plurimùm adjuverit; fuorum librorum plurimos mihi dedit, reliquorum liberum conceffit ufum, atque totum annum, dum fub prælo liber ifte erat (collegis humaniffimè affentientibus) hofpitio me accepit; quam humanitatem à Reverendiffimo Archiepifcopo, de quo priùs in ipsâ epiftolâ memini, benigniffimè oblatam, ut repudiarem, coegit Thamefis fluvius, illius domum à prælo dividens atque fejungens.

Sic

* Morgani fcilicet interpretationem, anno 1588.

Sic opem tulerunt non contemnendam

DAVID POWELUS, Sacræ Theologiæ Doctor.

EDMUNDUS PRICEUS, Archidiaconus Meirion.

RICHARDUS VACHANUS, Hofpitii Divi Joannis, quod eft Literurthæ, Præfectus.

N°. III.

Dedication prefixed to the Bible printed in 1620.

Sacrofanctæ et Individuæ Trinitati, Uni Deo Optimo Maximo, Nominis Sanctificationem; JACOBO, Dei ejufdem gratiâ, Magnæ Britanniæ, Franciæ, et Hiberniæ Regi Auguftiffimo, felicitatem omnem precatur creatura humilis, fubditus fidelis.

QUI unâ tantùm ætate vivit, brevem; qui ingratus, miferam; qui fibi foli, parcam; quique otiofus, verè nullam vitam agit. Hic enim vivens mortuus eft, et memoria ejus perit cum eo. Idcircò ego, grati in Deum et Regem animi teftimonium, conterraneis commodum, meque vermem non hominem in terris repentem, benè, pro facultatulâ,

VERSIONS OF THE BIBLE. 113

tulâ, Ecclefiæ Chrifti voluiffe, indicium aliquod relinquere concupivi. Ad hæc nihil in fe dignius, Deo & Regi, ut rebar, gratius, Britannis ad falutem accommodatius, me facere poffe credidi, quàm fi id pro virili conarer in Britannicâ Bibliorum verfione, quod feliciter factum eft in Anglicanâ; et nunc præfertim, Bibliis, in plerifque apud nos Ecclefiis, aut deficientibus aut tritis; et nemine, quantùm audire potui, de excudendis novis cogitante.

Penè me ab inftituto terruit illud B. Hieronymi de opere fuo confimili: *Periculofum opus certè eft, et obftrectatorum latratibus patens* (a); & illud ejufdem: *Non parum eft fcire quid nefcias. Prudentis hominis eft nôffe menfuram fuam, nec imperitiæ fuæ cunctum orbem teftem facere* (b). Verùm hæfitantem animavit illud Domini ad Mofem: *Ego adero ori tuo.* Exod. iv. 12. Et illud ad Apoftolum: *Virtus mea in infirmitate*

(a) In Præfatione in Pentateuch. de Tranflatione fuâ.
(b) Adverfus Vigilantium.

infirmitate perficitur (d). Tuo igitur, Gratiofe Deus, auxilio fretus, & tuo, Rex, mandato Anglis (ut ad laudem pietatis veftræ teftantur) dato incitatus, necnon pio Reverendorum Præceflorum exemplo adductus ; viz. Richardi Davies, primò Afaphenfis, poftea Menevenfis Epifcopi, qui (auxiliante Gulielmo Salefburio) Novum Teftamentum; & Gulielmi Morgani, Afaphenfis nuper Epifcopi, qui Sacra Biblia fermone Britannico in lucem edidit. Ad illorum tranflationes, noviffimam præfertim, manus movi; atque, ubi opus videbatur, tanquàm vetus ædificium, novâ curâ inftaurare cœpi.

Quid igitur? ut inquit Hieronymus, *Damnamus Veteres? Minimè; fed poft illorum ftudia, in domo Domini quod poffumus, laboramus* (e). Licita poft vindemiam racematio, poft Meffem Spicarum collectio; & in ædificio cum laude conditoris ad faftigium perducto, licebit farta tecta curare, fuperflua tollere, collapfa reftaurare, malè hærentia connectere. Quemadmodùm igitur Athenienfes navigium

(d) 2 Cor. xii. 9. (e) Præfat. in Pentat.

VERSIONS OF THE BIBLE. 115

gium Thefei confervarunt, *ligna vetuſtate confecta tollentes, firmiora ſufficientes, atque ita coagmentantes, ut navem, alii eandem, alii non eandem eſſe contenderent* *; ſimilitèr ego certè quædam cum Præceſſoris laude retinui; quædam in Dei nomine mutavi, atque ſic compegi; ut et hìc fit ἀμφιδοξεμενον παραδειγμα, & dictu fit difficile, num vetus an nova, Morgani an mea, dicenda fit verſio.

Cujuſcunque fit, tua primò, Deus, eſt; ex quo, per quem, & in quem funt omnia. Nos enim fiſtulæ, tuus eſt ſpiritus; Tu Auctor, nos organa, per quæ Britanni, fuâ quâ nati funt linguâ, audiunt Dei magnalia. *Homo dextram porrigit, ſed Deus manum gubernat* (g); ergò quodcunque eſt benè, noſtris manibus, ſed tuis viribus factum eſt. In hoc non fum iniquus in te, non modò Regum Auguſtiſſime, ſed virorum optime, quòd tibi

(F) Τὰ παλαιὰ τῶν ξύλων ὑφαιρῦνlες, ἀλλα δὲ ἐμβάλλοnlες ἴσχυρα, κ) συμπηγνῦνlες ἔlως, ὡςι ἀμφιδοξέμενον παράδειγμα τὸ πλοῖον εἶναι. Plutarchus in Theſeo.

(g) Chryſoſtomus de Receſſu ſuo ex Aſiâ.

tibi Deum, qui te fecit & præfecit, anteferam. *Nullius enim injuria eft, cui Deus Omnipotens antefertur* (h).

Poft Deum proximè, Rex, tua eft, qui neminem, nifi Deum, fuperiorem habes. Si vetus, tua eft jure hæreditario; fi nova, tua eft jure acquifito. Præterquàm enim quòd ego tuus fum cum cæteris fubditus, mea, qualis qualis eft, Majeftati Veftræ debetur induftria, propter fingularem veftram & omnimodò gratuitam erga me gratiam; erga me, inquam, homuncionem inopem, ab aulâ *alienum, ruri inter Britannorum reliquias commorantem*, quod fempèr & ubique agnofco humillimè, & cum omni gratiarum actione. Etfi ergò, nec quod debetur compenfari, nec quicquam à parvitate meâ, dignum Majeftate Veftrâ expectari poffit; fpero tamèn devotionis meæ voluntatem hoc conatu dignofci poffe. Cui fi detur, Deo & Regi placere, Britannis prodeffe, habeo quod fuit

in

(b) Ambrofii Ep. 30.

in votis primum, in opere ſtudium, &
erit, quamdiù vixero, folatium. Deus
is, qui folus fapiens & fummè miferi-
cors eſt, Te, Rex Sereniſſime, & Tuos
in folio, fubditos omnes in obſequio,
quàm feliciſſimè cuſtodiat, uſque ad
adventum Chriſti glorioſum; in quo
vos pacificè regentes, nos ex animo ob-
temperantes, cum venerit inveniat Is,
cujus eſt, cum Patre et Spiritu Sanɕto,
regnum, potentia, & gloria, in fecula
feculorum. Amen.

Richardus Afaphenſis.

HISTORICAL AND CRITICAL
REMARKS
ON THE
BRITISH TONGUE,
AND IT'S
CONNECTION
WITH OTHER
LANGUAGES,
founded on it's STATE in the
WELSH BIBLE.

PRINTED FIRST IN THE YEAR 1769.

To His Royal Highness

GEORGE
PRINCE OF WALES.

SIR,

BY patronizing a defign to fupport the neceffitous orphans of Ancient Britons, for whom the Law has made no provifion in London, Your ROYAL HIGHNESS has already fhown Your regard to the Principality. From this very early inftance of a readinefs to do them good, the natives of that country will infer a difpofition in future to countenance every attempt for their advantage worthy of encouragement. Prefuming upon this difpofition, fo flattering

to

to my views, I have ventured to folicit the patronage of the PRINCE of WALES for the following remarks, and more efpecially for the Language on which they are founded. The great condefcenfion and readinefs, with which the ambitious wifhes of the author in behalf of his work have been gratified, is hereby moft refpectfully acknowledged; but, for the fame readinefs to favour and patronize the Britifh tongue, Your ROYAL HIGHNESS may depend upon the applaufe and benediction of thoufands.

I am, SIR,
Your ROYAL HIGHNESS's
Moft obedient, devoted, and
Faithful, humble fervant,

Thomas Llewelyn.

HISTORICAL AND CRITICAL REMARKS ON THE BRITISH TONGUE, &c.

INTRODUCTION.

THE Britiſh tongue is a language, daily ſpoken by thouſands, and by hundreds of thouſands, in the Principality of Wales. It is a language, in which a conſiderable number of books have been compoſed and publiſhed. The Rev. Mr. Moſes Williams, a gentleman to whom his country is many ways indebted,

depicted, printed above fifty years ago a catalogue of books (a), publifhed relative to Wales, and moftly in the Welfh tongue; which catalogue contains the names, and fometimes brief accounts, of near two hundred books of different fizes. Since the printing of the above catalogue, feveral other books, both original compofitions and tranflations, have been publifhed in the fame language. Reading among the lower clafs of people is become much more common and general in that country now than formerly. Since the year 1737, two hundred and twenty thoufand perfons and upwards, we are informed (b), have been taught to read in one particular fort of fchools, called Circulating Welfh Charity Schools; firft fet up by the late
Rev.

(a) For the perufal of this curious and uncommon catalogue, I am obliged to my communicative friend, Richard Morris, Efq; the very worthy Prefident of the Cymmrodorion Society.

(b) Welfh Piety for the year 1768.

Rev. and truly pious Mr. Griffith Jones; and, since his death, supported by the voluntary contributions of well disposed persons. To those who are duly informed of this state and use of the language, remarks upon it need no apology.

As little occasion does there seem to be of any apology for founding these remarks in some measure on the British translation of the Scriptures. It was thought necessary to fix upon some state of the language for a proper foundation; and none seemed more fit for this purpose than the state of it in the Welsh Bible. The Bible is the common book of christians; it appears in the language of every Protestant country; in Wales especially, it is a principal book, the most known and the most read of any; and it has the best claim to be reckoned the standard for the language. To this, other publications, being mostly of a later date, accommodate themselves; and hence their stile derives it's manner and colouring. Tho' in general the supplies of this
book

book have not been adequate to the wants or demands of the people, yet at prefent they are in the way of procuring pretty ample provifion. A quarto impreffion with a fhort commentary, confifting of about ten thoufand copies is now printing by fubfcription at Carmarthen; and at the fame time, another edition in octavo, containing twenty thoufand books, is carrying on at London, under the patronage of the Society for promoting Chriftian Knowledge.

The following remarks are not of a fort; they are therefore divided in the enfuing treatife, and thrown into two feparate and diftinct parts.

Part the firft takes up the Britifh tongue in it's prefent ftate, and furveys it's general compleftion and features, as it appears in the Welfh Bible. With a view to the claims of the language to felf-fufficience and purity, it examines the terms or words of it in the grofs; and inquires whether they are original and

INTRODUCTION.

and native, or foreign and borrowed. It traces it's connection and intercourfe with other languages; and confiders what it has gained or fuffered by their means.

The fecond part enters more thoroughly into the genius and conftitution of the Welfh tongue; it refolves and analyfes it's feveral parts and materials; examines it's peculiar nature and properties; and inquires, how far it is regular, and after the manner of the Englifh and other languages; or wherein it remarkably varies and differs from others, whether ancient or modern; and with all the concifenefs, of which the author was mafter, confiftent with clearnefs, it points out the advantages or difadvantages of the Britifh, for compofition, and for eafe and ftrength of expreffion.

A long difufe of the language had well nigh totally difqualified the writer, and rendered him almoft quite inferior to fuch an attempt. He was moft fenfibly affected with the profpect of the difficulties in the fecond part, and thereby

like

like to have been deterred entirely from taking it in hand. If in the execution of it, attempted notwithſtanding, any material miſtakes are committed, it is hoped that this conſideration will be admitted as ſome extenuation of his defects; and that his well meant endeavour, tho' it may be deficient and in ſome inſtances erroneous, will yet be acceptable in the main, and of real ſervice to his country.

OBSERVATIONS on languages are commonly dry and abſtruſe, or elſe run in rough and uneaſy channels. It is too ſeldom that they contain much of what is new and worth knowing; and ſeldomer ſtill that they afford any thing very entertaining. But remarks on the Britiſh tongue cannot be expected to go in a known and beaten track; and they muſt at leaſt have the character of novelty to recommend them. The attempt is undoubtedly new; and it is believed that the ſubject is capable of throwing ſome

new

new light on the nature of languages in general. The author has wifhed to be able to handle the fubject in fuch a manner as might yield information without being tedious, not only to his countrymen, but to thofe alfo who are unacquainted with the language, on which thefe remarks are founded. How far he has fucceeded in the attempt, and accomplifhed his wifhes, muft be left to others in due time to determine.

The fate of languages, like that of feveral eminent perfons, has been a good deal unfortunate. Living, they are neglected and flighted; but dead, they are commended and decorated with all the ornaments of learning and eloquence. The Englifh, the living language of Great Britain, &c. fpoken daily by millions, has yet been lefs ftudied in Britain, than the Greek tongue, which is fpoken by nobody; and the Britifh, another living language of thoufands in this land, has yet been as little or lefs cultivated here than the Arabick. Englifh writers of the firft character have remonftrated againft fuch a conduct, in behalf of the Englifh tongue; and have recommended to their countrymen the cultivation and thorough knowledge of their own language. In the fame manner, I could wifh to recommend to every inhabitant of Wales, the right underftanding of his Mother tongue. While it is yet alive, and in daily ufe, let it be ftudied and cultivated; and fhould it ever be it's fate to be reckoned among the dead, may it then meet with the ufual treatment and honours of dead languages!

THE FIRST PART.

Effect of other languages on the British tongue.

CHAP. I.

Ancient state and extent of the British language.

WE are informed by the Venerable Bede (a), that in his time five different languages were used in common by the several inhabitants of this island: these five were the English, the British, the Scotish, the Pictish, and the Latin.

(a) Eccles. Hist. beginning.

This was about a thoufand years ago. For a long while this number has been reduced to three, the Welfh, the Erfe and the Englifh; or rather, if the two firft be only different dialects of one and the fame language, the prefent number will be two, the Britifh and the Englifh. The laft, though the youngeft, is at this day by far the moft general and extenfive. The other, though now confined within narrower limits, is yet much the moft ancient; and was very probably in former days more general and extenfive than the Englifh is now, or perhaps any other modern European tongue.

Two thoufand years ago, the ftate of languages, in thefe weftern parts of the world, feems to have been much more fimple and uniform than at prefent. The Britifh alone was ufed through England, Scotland, Wales and Ireland; and, as fhould feem likely, it was the general, the common language of great part of the continent befides. It feems to have been

been the language of the ancient Celtæ, as well as of the ancient Britons; and thefe Celtæ, under different denominations, fpread themfelves over feveral countries of Europe. We find them in France, in Italy, and in Spain, under the different names of Belgæ, Galli, Celtæ and Celtiberi. In Germany, and more eafterly and northerly, they went under the appellations of Cimbri, Cimmerii, &c. And we read of fome of their fettlements as far as Greece and Afia minor (b).

If ever the Britifh tongue thus generally prevailed, in fuch different climes, and in fuch diftant countries; it is fcarce poffible, that it fhould have been every where quite uniform and alike. It muft have been diverfified and broken into numberlefs varieties and dialects. But what thefe dialects were, or what their peculiarities, we know not.

As Britain itfelf in thofe days was divided into a multitude of little ftates and principalities;

(b) Hiftoire des Celtes par Pelloutier.

principalities; the language of it's inhabitants could not have been entirely similar and uniform. Subjects of different kingdoms and provinces, especially when they have but little correspondence with each other, will have different dialects and varieties of speech. We find this frequently to happen in different counties, in no distant parts of the same country, and under the same government.

If the ancient inhabitants of this island had ever any considerable intercourse with Phœnicians, Carthaginians, or other foreigners of a speech quite different from their own; they would then in all probability adopt some foreign words or expressions, and incorporate them with their own stock. But of this also we have no full and certain account. And supposing such an event to have happened; words thus adopted, at a period so distant, could not now be distinguished from the native and original terms of the language.

Those

Thofe times are too obfcure; too remote for our reach. In hundreds of inftances, they leave us uncertain and diffatisfied in our inquiries; we muft therefore defcend lower down, and to much later times, ere we arrive at the due diftance, or fix ourfelves in the proper ftation, whence we may be able to diftinguifh; whether there be any thing exotick and adventitious in the compofition of this tongue; and which of it's words are natives, or which are foreign.

In defcending for this purpofe fo low as the time of the Reformation, and in confidering the ftate of this fubject as it ftands in the Welfh Bible; we fhall take the language at a confiderable difadvantage. The Welfh Bible is not an original compofition, but a tranflation; and tranflations can hardly be expected as pure and unmixed as original compofitions. It is alfo the tranflation of a book of a peculiar kind, where the fame liberty muft not be taken as in tranflating books of a different fort. It is further, a tranflation undertaken and accomplished with fewer helps, and under more difadvantages, than moft other verfions of the fame book (c). Due and proper allowances therefore fhould be made for thefe circumftances, while we attend to this fubject, and examine how far the language of this verfion may have been affected by intermixtures from other tongues.

THE languages which may be fuppofed to have had any effect in this cafe muft be; either the original languages of the Old and New Teftament, whence the tranflation was made; or the languages which at different times have prevailed in this country, and muft have affected the language of it's original inhabitants. Each of thefe will be found to have had fome fhare in this matter.

C H A P.

(c) Hiftorical account of the Britifh verfions and editions of the Bible.

CHAP. II.

Effect of the Hebrew language.

TOGETHER with the Greek, the Latin, the Englifh, and perhaps all other tranflations of the Old Teftament; the Britifh verfion feems, in certain cafes, to have acquired fomething of a Hebrew phrafeology and turn of expreffion.

Yn y dydd y bwyttêi di o hono, *gan farw y byddi farw*, in the Welfh Bible, Gen. ii. 17. in the day thou eateft thereof, *dying thou fhalt die*, in the margin to the fame paffage in Englifh, are expreffions which found well, and convey a ftrong and full meaning in both languages. They are not however in the ftile of Britifh legiflation, nor of the laws of Howel Dda; and fo in a great many other fimilar inftances where the

Hebrew

Hebrew idiom and manner is preserved in our tranflation.

It has further adopted and retained multitudes of fingle words from the Hebrew language. Befides long catalogues, and almoft whole books in the Old Teftament, containing little more than the Hebrew proper names of different perfons and families; it retains *Cerub*, *Eden*, *Jehova*, *Sabbath*, and many others, which are mere Hebrew words untranflated, only difguifed by being clothed in common letters. But thefe Hebrew terms and turns of expreffion ought not to be efteemed as defects in this tranflation, at leaft not as peculiar to it, feeing they are to be met with in every verfion of the Old Teftament; and even to a confiderable extent in the original Greek of the New. And it might have been deemed an idle affectation in our tranflators to have attempted avoiding them.

Excepting terms of this caft, and perhaps fome few others, fuch as *Aber*, *Caer*,

Caer, *Sâch*, &c. we have, as far as I can find, hardly any words in the Britifh tongue of clear Hebrew compleftion and affinity.

Suppofing the Hebrew to have been the original language of mankind, and the common parent of all other tongues, as is generally fuppofed; in that cafe numbers of common words, evidently of Hebrew parentage, might be expefted to appear in this, and in every other verfion of the Old Teftament. But if we entertain fuch an expectation we fhall be difappointed. And whoever compares a chapter or a page of the Hebrew Bible with the correfponding page or chapter in the Greek, in the Latin, in the Englifh, in the Welfh, or perhaps in any other European verfion; whoever, I fay, will be at the pains to make fuch a comparifon, will be able to difcover the plain and certain origin of but very few words.

It is commonly faid, that the Britifh and the Hebrew are fimilar languages;

but

but by this muſt be underſtood, not that they ſeem to be derived the one from the other, or that there are a great many radical words the ſame in each; but only that there is a ſimilarity of ſound in certain letters of both alphabets; that they are alike in ſome peculiarities of conſtruction, eſpecially in the change incident to ſeveral letters in the beginning of words. If any thing farther is intended hereby, it will be more, I believe, than can be warranted and ſupported by a fair compariſon of the two languages.

C H A P.

CHAP. III.

EFFECT OF THE GREEK TONGUE.

THE Britifh verfion, together with the Latin, the Englifh, and moft other tranflations of fcripture, has adopted and retained, with little variation, feveral words from the Greek tongue. Thefe it derives from the feptuagint verfion of the Old Teftament, and from the original language of the New. Hence Bible itfelf, the general title for the whole book, and Apocrypha for a principal divifion of it. Hence *Genefis* and *Exodus*, *Chronicles* and *Pfalms*, and the names of many other particular books of the Old Teftament. Hence a great many words of various forts throughout that part of fcripture, and it may be yet more in the New Teftament. Hence *Angel, Apoftol, Efengyl, Eglwys,* and
multitudes

multitudes of other terms peculiar to facred and theological fubjects; and thefe words of Greek extraction and affinity will be found to be much more numerous than thofe of Hebrew origin, in every verfion of the Bible for thefe weftern parts of the world.

WHATEVER tongue may have been the primitive and original language of the human race; the Greek feems to have been the moft general and diffufive of any, and to have had the moft univerfal effect upon other languages. It feems to have been the parent language of fciences and of arts, at leaft to have been the principal vehicle of their communication and conveyance through the world. And we find in the Bible, in treatifes upon almoft every fubject, and alfo in feveral occupations and employments of life, abundance of words evidently borrowed from this tongue. Thefe are in general technical terms, or words peculiar to arts and particular profeffions. Thofe ufed

in

in the Bible are principally of a peculiar nature and fignification, and, like the proper terms of arts or fciences, ought to be retained through the various verfions of fcripture, and indeed through every treatife on thofe fubjects to which fuch terms relate.

Befides thefe appropriated words, if I may fo call them, liberally furnifhed by the Greek tongue, for the prefervation and improvement of arts and of knowledge; there are others of Greek features and complection, of a ftill more general and extenfive nature, which are found to be interfperfed in great numbers through many or moft of the languages of Europe.

The Grecians are faid to have been the anceftors of the Romans, and the Greek tongue the parent of the Latin ; and the Latin has been generally ready to acknowledge it's obligation, and to claim the Greek for it's mother tongue.

French authors, in behalf of their nation, have claimed affinity with the Greeks,

Greeks, and from that language have derived a confiderable part of their own.

The Englifh alfo has been deduced from the fame fource. Through the Saxon, it's more immediate anceftor, it has been traced up to the Teutonick or Gothick — languages ufed in the neighbourhood of the Greek, and of the fame compleƈtion and kindred (d).

Others have put in the like claim in behalf of the Celtick or Britifh, which they affirm to be equally if not more nearly related to the Greek; and upon a comparifon of both tongues together, feveral inftances appear of a ftriking refemblance, not to fay of famenefs. Pezron has publifhed a pretty large catalogue of words of this make: fuch as, αηρ, *awyr*, air; ϐρυν, *bron*, breaft; γενειον, *gên*, chin; ὑδωρ, *dwr*, water, &c (e).

Thefe

(d) Clark on ancient weights and money.
(e) Antiquities of nations, book the third.

Thefe and other Greek and Britifh words are fo much alike, that they coincide in found and in fignification, and are evident proofs of a very ancient affinity between thefe two tongues. How and when fuch a relation commenced may not now appear.

It is eafy to fay the Britons borrowed thefe terms from the Greeks; but it is not fo eafy to fhow the correfpondence between the two nations, by means of which fuch a loan might be negotiated in Greece, and the goods imported to this ifland. Befides this, the above words are the moft unlikely of any to have ever been borrowed. Perfons, the fondeft for borrowing, never borrow their legs or arms; nor is it probable, that they fhould ever borrow the words by which thefe things are fignified.

Every language and people muft have them from the beginning. They cannot do without them, any more than they can fubfift without air or water, or live deftitute of the moft effential parts and
members

members of their own bodies. It muft feem, therefore, moft reafonable to conclude, not that one of thefe tongues is derived from the other, but that they are both kindred languages, and proceed from one common origin.

Befides Hebrew and Greek terms, communicated by the two original languages of fcripture; the Britifh language, and the Britifh verfion of the Bible, have feveral words in common with thofe foreign tongues, which, at different times, have prevailed in this ifland. The firft of this clafs, and that which has had the moft general and extenfive influence, is the Latin.

C H A P.

CHAP. IV.

Effect of the Latin Tongue.

THE Romans, as hiftory informs us, were the firft invaders and foreign oppreffors of this country. The Latin tongue was their language, and, with their arms, was extended over a confiderable part of the terraqueous globe. It was ufed in Britain for fome centuries; if not by the natives, yet by foreign legions and colonifts, when Britain made a part of the Roman empire. When that huge and unweildy body crumbled to pieces, when the power of that people was broken and abolifhed, their language maintained it's ground, and fpread even yet farther. The Latin tongue became the general language of the church of Rome, and of the publick exercifes of religion in every country where that church was eſtabliſhed. It became the language of ſchools, of ſenates, and of courts of law. It became the language of the learned in moſt countries in Europe, and the vehicle of all ſorts of knowledge for hundreds of years. It became, in a ſenſe, alſo the language of the unlearned, of numbers who underſtood not a word of it, wherein they were required to tranſact with God and with men the moſt important of their concerns. It is not at all ſurpriſing therefore, that this language ſhould have formed a conſiderable part of almoſt every European tongue; that it ſhould have become a principal ingredient in the compoſition of the French, of the Italian, and of other languages on the continent, and likewiſe intermix itſelf with thoſe uſed in the different parts of this iſland.

It has intermixed itſelf with the Engliſh, and conſtitutes a main part, perhaps the moſt expreſſive and ſubſtantial part, of that tongue. It has alſo undoubtedly affected the Welſh tongue, and

and introduced into the Welſh Bible words, which would never have appeared in it, had it not been for the connections between this country and the Roman empire, or the church of Rome.

From the Latin it has borrowed the name of diſtinction for the principal diviſion of the Bible into Old and New Teſtament. To this tongue it ſtands indebted for *Actau* and *Numeri,* names of particular books in each of theſe Teſtaments; and from the ſame ſource it has derived *appelio, condemno, ffurfafen, tabernacl, teml,* and ſuch like.

The diſtinction made above, with regard to words of Greek complection, will equally apply to words of Latin features and affinity. Some of them are evidently derivatives; but they are appropriated terms, peculiar to ſuch and ſuch ſubjects; and muſt be made uſe of, whenever we treat on thoſe ſubjects to which they belong. Others are of a more general nature and application; ſtand for things the moſt eſſential to man,

man, and the moft common in nature; and are utterly incompatible with all ideas of lending and borrowing; and however they may refemble words of other languages, both in found and in fenfe, yet they can never be thought to have been derived or borrowed from them, by fuch as duly attend to this matter. Yet of this clafs are numbers of thofe terms, ufually reckoned derivatives from the Latin. Thus *Corph* and *Corpus*, *Braich* and *Brachium*, *Dant* and *Dens*, the correfponding words in each tongue for *Body*, for an *Arm*, and for a *Tooth*, are evidently fimilar terms, and muft have proceeded from the fame fpring; but they cannot be fuppofed to have been borrowed by one tongue from the other, any more than the things they fignify, can be thought to have been borrowed by one people from the other.

SOME curious perfons have pretended to give us the exact proportion between

tween the original words of the Welsh language, and those words which it has borrowed from other tongues. Dr. E. Bernard tells us (f), that one half of the words in Dr. Davies's dictionary are of Latin origin. Mr. E. Llwyd, on the other hand, says (g), that the number of Latin words in this estimate is fixed too high; and that the true proportion between them and others in that dictionary, is nearly the proportion of one to seven. The difference is considerable; but

Non est nostri tantas componere lites.

I shall only take the liberty to observe, that Dr. Bernard was undoubtedly a learned man, but no Cambro-briton; probably no master of the Welsh tongue; and judged only by resemblance,

and

(f) Letter to Dr. Hickes at the end of Islandick grammar, quarto edition.

(g) Nicholson's Engl. Hist. Library, page 29.

and by a random eſtimate. He wrote his letter to Dr. Hickes in 1689. In 1693, according to the Biographia Britannica and A. Wood, he married a beautiful young lady, deſcended from ſome of the princes of Wales; after which he perhaps thought otherwiſe of this matter; and though he *publiſhed* no formal recantation, the above letter was ſuppreſſed, and not ſuffered to be reprinted with the Iſlandick grammar, on the republication of it in Hickes's works.

Mr. E. Llwyd may have been equally learned, and a Briton. He was a perfect maſter of his native tongue, and took the pains to reckon up all the words in Davies's dictionary. He makes them to amount to about ten thouſand, of which about fifteen hundred, ſomewhat leſs than a ſeventh part, he owns, might be like the Latin. But without aiming at mathematical exactneſs, in a ſubject ſo vague and uncertain, if we compare together a ſingle chapter or
paragraph

paragraph of the Welſh and of the Latin Bible, we may ſee reaſon to ſuſpect that even E. Llwyd's eſtimate is fixed full high. In the firſt chapter of Geneſis in Welſh, I queſtion whether there be a dozen words of evident Latin reſemblance, or half a dozen in the firſt Pſalm.

CHAP.

CHAP. V.

Effect of the English language.

THE Englifh, or the Saxon, is another tongue, by which the Britifh language, and the Britifh verfion of the fcriptures, may be fuppofed to have been affected.

Next to the Romans, the Saxons invaded this country, and oppreffed and plundered it's original inhabitants. If we may depend on the account commonly given of their arrival here, they came into this ifland at firft, as friends and auxiliaries. They were invited over, not to ftay a few weeks, like a party of Heffians, or Hanoverians, but to remain for a time, like and inftead of Roman legions, for continued protection and defence. Coming hither at firft in this manner, we may fuppofe that

that, for a while, they would intermix with the natives, and accommodate themselves to their manners and cuftoms. How long any friendly intercourfe fubfifted, and particularly what effect fuch an intercourfe might have upon the language of either people, cannot at prefent be afcertained.

When the Saxons, inftead of auxiliaries, became the enemies of the Britons; — even after they had plundered the natives of the greateft and beft part of their country; all correfpondence between the two nations doth not feem to have been wholly and conftantly cut off. In the time of the heptarchy, we find the Britons affifting fome of the Saxon kings againft others of the fame race. When England became a monarchy, it's fubjects and it's fovereigns appeared to have vifited the principality on feveral occafions. And ftill more, the two nations have now been one kingdom near five hundred years: a period confiderably longer than that

that, in which the Romans remained in this country.

In all this time it may seem impoffible but the language of each muft have been affected. Not only the names of perfons, of places, and of fome peculiar fubjects, would become common to both people; but feveral other words and modes of expreffion would be adopted by one from the other, and added to it's own ftock. Accordingly, we find in each language feveral words of this fort; though they are not near fo numerous as thofe, which both have in common with the Latin; and it may be difficult to determine, in particular inftances, to which of the two fuch common words did originally belong.

DR. BERNARD, as referred to above, gives them all the honour of an Englifh extraction, and affures us, that they make a fourth part of the words in Dr. Davies's dictionary. Mr. Llwyd again took the pains to reckon them, and

and on the contrary depofes, that they make only about one in fifty of the words in that book;—inftead of five and twenty hundred, which make a quarter part of it's number of ten thoufand, they hardly amount to two hundred; and even this reduced number he will not allow to be all of Englifh parentage and defcent, only like the Englifh, of doubtful pedigree and birth, fome from one language, and the reft from the other.

This is a very great difference, and fhows the uncertainty of the fubject, as well as the tendency and difpofition of the writers. It is rather an affair of curiofity than of importance; it does not feem capable of much precifion, nor to be of, weight enough to require it; general and probable conjectures may be as much as can be expected; and even thefe conjectures will be different, according to the different ftate of the language, with a
view

view to which they may be particularly formed.

Take the language of Wales as used in converfation, efpecially on the borders, and you will find it to be part Welfh and part Englifh, abounding with Englifh words under a Welfh form. But take the fame language as ufed by fome authors, particularly as ufed in the Bible, and you will find it to make a very different appearance. Words of refemblance in the Welfh and Englifh will be but few; fome there are, but not near the quantity which might have been expected; they are to be found in the greateft number in the firft edition of the New Teftament; we there meet with feveral words of plain Englifh or Saxon derivation: as, from the Englifh *courteous*, that tranflation had *cwrtais* for *addfwyn*; from *unprofitable* it had *amproffitiol*, inftead of *anfuddiol*; inftead of *Grawn win*, it had *grabs* for *grapes*; and inftead of *goruchwilwr*, *fteward*.

Thefe

These have been corrected in subsequent impressions; and there may be still room for some farther amendment, and to strike out *cwmfforddus, concwerwr, happus,* words of clear Saxon complection and features; and to give in lieu thereof *cyssurus, gorchfygwr, dedwydd,* terms of equivalent signification, but of more genuine British complection, and more consonant with the rest of the language. Should this be done, English derivatives will stand very rare in that book, much thinner than such as are plainly analogous to the Latin; which will appear the more surprising, when we reflect on the length of time, in which the English has been the general language of this country, considerably more than one thousand years; when we reflect that England and Wales have been one kingdom near half of that period; and when we reflect also on the number of English words continually used by the inhabitants of Wales, especially on the borders. But,

ROMANS

Romans and Saxons have not been the only foreigners who invaded this country, or deprived it's inhabitants of their rights and liberties. Danes followed the example which others had fet them; they difturbed and haraffed the Saxons, fcarce warm in their feats, and long infefted and plundered every part of the kingdom. And after them the Normans invaded and oppreffed the Englifh, and fettled themfelves in their poffeffions. As to the languages of thefe foreigners, it does not appear that the Danifh tongue had any great effect on any of thofe ufed in this ifland. But the Norman language had an effect which was very extenfive and lafting.

In Normandy, duke William and his fubjects made ufe of the French tongue; when he became conqueror and king of England, we are told by fome of his hiftorians that he attempted to learn the language of this country; and when he found he could not mafter it, he wanted to deftroy it, and to introduce

duce and eftablifh the French in it's place. Though in this attempt he did not fucceed entirely to his wifhes, yet he brought his native tongue to be much in ufe. He dictated his laws and ordinances in that language; he commanded his Englifh fubjects to learn, and not fail to make ufe of it on feveral occafions. In confequence of this, probably, charters, pleadings, and ftatutes of this realm, have been drawn up in the French tongue; and this has had a confiderable effect on the Englifh language, and given it in many inftances a French or Gallick air and complection; but it does not appear to have had any effect on the language of Wales. A party of Normans, it is faid, feized upon Glamorganfhire, foon after the Conqueft; and fome of the defcendants of this party may remain there to this day; but I know of no traces of their tongue in any part of that county; and the Welfh Bible feems to be entirely

entirely free from every taint or mixture of this kind.

Such, in general, has been the effect of foreign tongues on the Britifh, and on the ftile and language of the Welfh Bible. It has admitted fome words from the Hebrew and Greek tongues, and thefe feem to have been neceffary and unavoidable, and did not proceed from any peculiar fcantinefs or penury of the language. All other tranflations have done the fame, and even the originals themfelves have acted upon the fame principle. For there are Greek terms intermixed with the Hebrew of the Old Teftament, and fome Latin among the Greek of the New. It has admitted fome words alfo from the Latin and the Englifh, neighbour languages, which have long prevailed in this ifland. It has made a more frequent and more plentiful ufe of the former; but it has admitted the latter

very

very feldom, and with a fparing hand. But,

There is another refpect in which it has been affected by one or both the other languages laft mentioned; that is, it's alphabet or letters have, as far as appears, been always nearly the fame with the Latin or Englifh; I do not mean as to the found of the letters, but as to their form or character.

CHAP. VI.

Effect of the Latin Alphabet.

WHEN letters, or alphabetical writing, were firſt introduced among the ancient Britons, or what characters they uſed in the beginning, doth not appear.

Ceſar tells us (h), that, in and before his time, Greek letters or characters were uſed by the Gauls, the neareſt neighbours of the Britons, with whom they had maintained long and frequent intercourſe.

Another author ſays (i), that the ſame letters were uſed in Britain, and that the Druids in particular were well acquainted with the Greek tongue.

Under the word alphabet, in Roſtrenen's

(h) Bell. Gall. lib. 6. c. 14.
(i) Ellingü Hiſt. Græc. Ling. pag. 257.

.ſtrenen's French and Celtick dictionary, is printed a complete ſet of characters taken from old inſcriptions, found in Bretaigne in France, and called by the author "the alphabet of the ancient "Armorick Bretons." Though theſe inſcriptions are undoubtedly poſterior to the introduction of Chriſtianity, being found on chalices, croſſes, and ſuch like monuments; they may yet exhibit an alphabet of a more early date, — poſſibly the alphabet once generally uſed by the ancient inhabitants of Gaul and Britain.

However that be, when the Britons became ſubject to the Romans, they adopted the Latin characters or alphabet, as appears from inſcriptions, and legends of money, then coined in this country.

The oldeſt Britiſh manuſcripts extant appear in what is called the Saxon or the Anglo-Saxon character (k).

And

(k) Archai. Britan. pages 7, and 225.

The Anglo-Saxon character is ſuppoſed by ſome

to

And printed books in that language have in general made ufe of the Englifh types and characters of the times; in the fixteenth century they appear in what is called the black letter; and fince then in the more common Englifh or Roman.

But the Latin or Englifh alphabet does not cleverly bend and accommodate itfelf to the temper and genius of the Britifh tongue. It is fometimes redundant, affording two or three characters for one found; all which, except one,

to have been that ufed by the Saxons while in Germany, and brought with them to this ifland. But by others, who think the Saxons had no knowledge of letters, before they came over to Britain, this character has been fuppofed to have been the alphabet of the Britons, and from them adopted by the Saxons;—but on a very flight examination we fhall find it no diftinct alphabet, but the fame with the Latin, only varied a little in about fix or eight letters.

one, are rejected by the Welſh. In other inſtances it is as deficient, and obliges us to join two or three characters to expreſs one ſimple Britiſh ſound. Several attempts have therefore been made to reform this alphabet, and to match it better to the Welſh tongue.

In order to underſtand the nature of theſe attempts, I will here lay before the reader the following table, exhibiting at one view the ſeveral alphabets, which appear to have been uſed at different times by the different inhabitants of this iſland.

To bring the following alphabets within the compaſs of one page, the j and the q, two Latin and Engliſh letters, are omitted.

The laſt letter in the fourth column is a make ſhift of the printer for a ſtrange character, of which he had no type. So is the Greek dipthong ȣ in the ſame column a little higher up. The ſame is to be underſtood alſo of the ſame characters, where they occur in the body of the book. The Saxon types likewiſe are but indifferent, and ſeem to require ſome ſuch apology.

WELSH TONGUE.

						Sound
a	a	a	a	a	a	
b	b	b	b	b	b	Eng. v.
—	—	—	bh	—	—	
c	c	c	c	—	—	peculiar
—	—	ch	ch	χ	χ	[*th* in the]
d	ð	d	d	d	d	
—	—	dd	dh	dh	ð	
e	e	e	e	e	e	Eng. v.
—	—	f	—	—	—	
f	ꝼ	ff	—	f	ꝼ	
g	ʒ	g	g	ʒ	g	
—	—	ng	gh	ʒh	ʒ	*ng* in King
—	—	—	ghh	—	—	
h	h	h	h	h	h	
i	i	i	i	i	i	
k	k	—	—	k	k	
l	l	l	l	l	l	
—	—	ll	lh	lh	λ	peculiar
m	m	m	m	m	m	
—	—	—	mh	—	—	
n	n	n	n	n	n	
—	—	—	nh	—	—	
o	o	o	o	o	o	
p	p	p	p	p	p	
—	—	ph	ph	—	—	Greek φ
r	ꞃ	r	r	r	r	
—	—	rh	rh	rh	ꞃ	
s	ſ	s	s	s	ſ	
—	—	—	—	ſh	—	
t	τ	t	t	t	t	
—	þ	th	th	th	τ	*th* in thro'
u	ü	u	u	—	—	
v	—	—	—	v	v	
w	p	w	ȝ	u	u	
x	x	—	—	—	—	
y	ẏ	y	y	y	y	
—	—	—	ẏ	ẏ	ẏ	
z	z	—	—	z, zh	z, zh	

The feveral alphabets in this table are plainly of a family, and derive from one common head. The firft column contains the Latin, or if you will the Englifh, which is exactly the fame. The fecond contains the Saxon, differing only in a few characters. The third exhibits the common Britifh or Welfh. In the fourth row are the improvements of the third, propofed by Dr. Rhŷs. And in the fifth and fixth, two other amendments of the fame, propofed and recommended by Mr. E. Llwyd;—the firft, given by himfelf in the fecond and the two hundred and twenty-fifth pages of the Archaiologia Britannica; and the other, deduced from his preface. A feventh column is added, giving the found of fome particular letters;—where nothing is fet down, the found nearly coincides with that of the Englifh or Latin.

One attempt to reform the common Welfh alphabet was made by Dr. John David Rhŷs, a learned phyfician in the
fixteenth

sixteenth century, and author of *Linguæ Cymraecæ Institutiones Accuratæ*, printed in 1592. This author rejects the f, the ff, and the w, of the common alphabet. He rejects also all doubling of the same letter: as, dd and ll; and instead of the w he substitutes a character like the Greek dipthong ȣ, and gives a character nearly of this form ү, for a sound some what resembling the y.

To compensate for the rejection of the double consonants, and to express more fully the different sounds of the letters, he adds an h to each consonant: thus; bh, ch, dh, gh, &c. through all the consonants in the alphabet, the s only excepted.

To exemplify and recommend this scheme, the author wrote a Welsh addrefs to his countrymen on his own plan, and prefixed it to the above book. But I do not find that he has ever been followed by any one person; and the addrefs itself has, I apprehend, been less read, as the language of it

seems

feems fo aukward and difguifed, that it is neither pleafant nor eafy to read it.

This attempt not fucceeding, Mr. E. Llwyd projected another method to new-model the alphabet of this language; and publifhed it in his Archaiologia Britannica, page the fecond, and again, more fully, page two hundred and twenty-five.

This learned and laborious writer banifhes the c, and calls back the k. He fubftitutes the Greek χ for the ch, and the Greek λ for the double l. He gives us the Englifh v for the fingle f, and affigns to this laft the found of the double f. Inftead of the g, or rather befides it, he introduces the Saxon ʒ, and other Saxon characters: as, b, ꝼ, p, r, τ and ẏ, for dd, ff, rh, s, th and y, the correfponding founds in the common alphabet. He expreffes the ng fometimes by ʒ, and fometimes by the fame character inverted Ƹ; and at times he adds an h to l, r, s, t and z: as, lh, rh, fh, th, and zh; and thus

makes

makes a medley, contradictory alphabet, confifting of Englifh, Saxon and Greek characters; with all which it is neceffary to be acquainted, before you can read his dedication AT Y KYMRY, prefixed to his book. This addrefs, like J. D. Rhŷs's dedication, has been, I believe, hardly ever imitated, and perhaps but feldom read; the language of it is fo greatly altered and disfigured; and befides this, the author himfelf is not fteady and uniform to his own plan. In the two pages of the Archaiologia Britannica, twice referred to already, he gives us one fort of alphabet; and he ufes another very different in the above mentioned dedication.

I know of no other projects for this fort of reformation, only the learned Dr. Davies ufed and recommended the ufe of ỿ, one of J. D. Rhŷs's characters; but even his recommendation and example has not been able to bring it into general practice; and all attempts to change letters once introduced,
though

though in many inftances wrong and defective, have yet been generally ineffectual. Even Roman emperors, who would fain have introduced only one or two new characters into the Latin alphabet, found they had not author ty enough to make them current: fo powerful, fo prevalent is cuftom, though ever fo wrong ; —

Penes quem eft jus & norma loquendi.

The Welfh muft therefore endeavour to make themfelves eafy as to this matter, and continue to make ufe of the types and characters of the times. The tranflators and editors of the Britifh Bible took thefe as they found them, though they were not in all refpects fo well adapted to their purpofe. Thus, the New Teftament of 1567 appeared in the black letter, the common Englifh type or character of that period; and it made ufe of every letter of the Englifh alphabet. It admitted even in common words the k, the q, and the v: as in *llynku* inftead of *llyngcu*; *quilidd* inftead of *cywilydd*; and *cyvod* for *cyfod*; which letters, together with the j, the x, and the z, fhould be ufed as they fay, only in exotick or foreign words; and have therefore fince that time been difcontinued, and other charaćters introduced in their ftead. But obfervations, relative to this article, will fall in our way more naturally under the fecond part of this fubjeċt, to which it may be now full time to proceed.

THE SECOND PART.

Peculiar Genius and Regulations
of the British Tongue.

LANGUAGES as spoken are very fleeting and tranfitory things. They are mere aerial beings, created by the breath of man's mouth, and no sooner created than they ceafe to exift, and perifh for ever. Writing forms a body for thefe fpiritual, momentary beings; it makes them objects of fight and fubftance, and gives them ftability and duration. Their original appearance in this new created ftate was, moft probably, very rude and irregular, like the firft writings of a beginner,

ner, or the epiftles of an ignorant peafant, awkward figures, and bad or falfe language. Human art and application improved upon thefe rough fketches and effays; and time and opportunity reduced them to order, and made letters and languages become the fubjects of laws and of government.

But fuch good fortune has not happened alike to every tongue. Hitherto no bodies at all have been created for the words of various languages. They have never yet been reduced by writing to a firm and permanent ftate; and where they have been thus reduced and fettled, they have met with very different degrees of regulation and improvement. The fortune of the Britifh tongue, in this refpect, it is my intention to confider in this fecond part.

This, in general, is the fubject of grammar; but a profeffed grammar is not here intended. Grammars for this language have been publifhed already by by Dr. Davies, Mr. Gambold, Mr. Richards and others; to which I would would refer ſuch as deſire more particular information this way. That the reader however may have a clearer idea of the nature and ſtructure of this tongue, it will be neceſſary to deſcend to ſome grammatical diſtinctions.

The diſtinction into three parts, reſpecting letters, words and ſentences, ſeems to be the moſt comprehenſive, and the moſt natural diviſion of grammar. Letters are the firſt, the raw materials or elements of a language. Words, confiſting of one or more of theſe elements, are again only it's materials in a ſecond and more advanced ſtate. And a combination of theſe laſt, regularly and properly diſpoſed, conſtitutes a period or ſentence. As, under theſe ſeveral diviſions, the Welſh tongue has ſome remarkable peculiarities; I ſhall attend to each of them in the following chapters, and in the order juſt mentioned.

C H A P.

CHAP. I.

Peculiar genius of the British alphabet.

THIS alphabet confifts of twenty-eight letters;--feven vowels, and twenty one confonants.

The vowels are, a, e, i, o, u, w and y. The five firft are vowels both in Welfh and in Englifh; the two laft are in Englifh ufually reckoned confonants, but improperly; the y in Enlifh has exactly the found of the i, and is as much a vowel; and the double u is as much fo, as the fingle u; or rather, as it confifts of two u's, it is not a fingle, but a double vowel or dipthong.

The confonants are, b, c, ch, d, dd, f, ff, g, ng, h, l, ll, m, n, p, ph, r, rh (1),
 ſ, t

---

(1) Rh is not fet down as a diftinct letter in the grammars of Dr. Davies and Mr. Richards; but

ſ, t and th. The remaining Engliſh characters, j, k, q, v, x and z, are uſed only for foreign words.

Should any think that this ſubject is low, little, and diſparaging to criticiſm, let them duly . attend to what follows, and I am much miſtaken or they will be of a different opinion. I have nothing material and peculiar to obſerve here of the vowels; what follows therefore reſpects the conſonants and them only.

The diſtinction of them into ſingle and double is unknown to the Welſh. Through the manifold defect of the common alphabet, they have plenty of double characters, but properly ſpeaking no double ſounds; none compounded like the Greek ψ, or the Engliſh

---

but they both have it in their dictionaries, where the ſingle r has no place; which ſhows that, on their own ſcheme, it ought to have had a place in their alphabets.

glifh x, and capable of being refolved into two feparate and diftinct founds. Though the letters are double, the found is fimple, and only one.

The confonants might be divided in the Welfh, as in other languages, into mutes, and half vowels or liquids; but fuch a divifion would be attended with no great advantage.

A better divifion would be into labials, palatines, and linguals, or dentals, fo denominated from the organs of fpeech, by which they are founded. Labials, pronounced by the lips, are fix: b, f, ff, m, p and ph; or rather five, as the ff and ph are only one and the fame found. Palatines, pronounced by the palate or throat, are alfo five: c, ch, g, ng, and h. The linguals or dentals, founded between the tongue and the teeth, are ten: d, dd, l, ll, n, r, rh, f, t, and th. This diftinction is the more important, as letters of the fame organ are often changed into one another in feveral languages

languages, and in none more remarkably than in the Welsh.

But the principal and moſt uſeful diviſion of theſe conſonants would be into *initials* and *non-initials*; or into ſuch as begin radical Britiſh words, and ſuch as begin none of them.

Non-initials are ſeven: dd, f, ng, l, ph, r and th; and they have this remarkable property—they will not ſtand at the head of any word of the language in it's original ſtate; they are not to be found in their order in any Britiſh dictionary; and all the words of that tongue muſt be ſought for, under ſome of the other letters (m).

The initial conſonants are fourteen, and muſt again be divided into *mutable* and *immutable*.

Immutables are five: ch, ff, h, n, and ſ; they are in the main very ſteady and invariable; place them once in

---

(m) Some few words may be found under f, and l, but they are not reckoned radical Britiſh words.

in their proper ſtation, and they will maintain their ground, and give way to none.

The other nine, b, c, d, g, ll, m, p, rh, and t, are very properly called mutables, being at leaſt moſt of them exceeding variable and unſteady, frequently ſhifting their ſituation, and, proteus-like, aſſuming various ſhapes and appearances; ſome, two; ſome, three; and ſome, four different forms.

In the changes and variations of theſe mutables, lies a great part of the art and myſtery of this very peculiar tongue, the moſt curious perhaps, and the moſt delicate for it's ſtructure, of any language in the world.

This may ſeem a ſtrange expreſſion. I ſhould yet be very eaſy as to any charge of partiality or exaggeration on the account of it, if I could make the reader a perfect maſter of this ſubject; it's peculiarity muſt render it difficult; I will however attempt to explain the *nature* and *use* of it; and to this purpose I will transcribe from Dr. Davies's grammar the following scheme, which exhibits in one view the several changes of these letters.

Lit. Mutabiles	FORMA.			
	1 Primaria recta seu radicalis	2 Mollis	3 Liquida	4 Aspirata
Declinatio. 1 — C P T	Câr Pen Tâd	Gâr Ben Dâd	Nghâr Mhen Nhâd	Châr Phen Thâd
Declinatio. 2 B D G	Bara Duw Gwr	Fara Dduw wr	Mara Nuw Ngwr	
Declinatio. 3 Ll M Rh	Llaw Mam Rhâd	Law Fam Râd		

The learned author of the above table composed his British grammar in the Latin tongue; and to explain the nature of his scheme he uses Latin words and takes up the idea of declensions, well known in that language. He divides his table into three

three declenſions, and each declenſion into a certain number of forms or caſes. The mutable letters are here ranged in one column; they are thrown a little out of their alphabetical order, that they might be more conveniently ſorted and reduced to three declenſions or claſſes.

The firſt declenſion conſiſts of words beginning with c, p, or t, and appearing like nouns of ſo many terminations, under four different forms; or to keep cloſer to the idea of declenſions, in four ſeveral caſes: *Câr, Gâr, Nghâr, Châr*, &c.

Declenſion the ſecond conſiſts of words beginning with b, d, or g (making the ſecond form of the firſt declenſion) and appearing like triptotes, under three forms or caſes: *Bara, Fara, Mara*, &c.

The third declenſion again conſiſts of words beginning with three letters, ll, m, or rh, and appearing like diptotes,

totes, only in two cafes or forms: *Llaw, Law*; *Mam, Fam*, &c.

In every declenfion, the word in it's firft form is in it's abfolute ftate, and begins with it's primary or radical letter. From this ftate of the word every other form is deduced. The change is made *univerfally* into confonants of the fame organ, but of a fofter found: *ec, eg, eng*, &c.

The fecond form is common to all the declenfions; and it's characteriftick is *Mollis*, that is, the radical letter foftened: *Tâd, Dâd; Duw, Dduw*, &c. The third form extends only to the two firft declenfions; it's denomination is *Liquida*, implying a further degree of foftnefs, or fluidity in the found of it's initials: *Câr, Gâr, Nghâr* (n), &c. The fourth form is peculiar to the firft

(n) The motion of the found in this proceffion is eafy and regular, but the expreffion of it by *ngh* is not fo happy. The fame may be faid of fome other characters ufed in thefe mutations.

firſt declenſion; and it's characteriſtick is *Aſpirata*, that is, the radical initial, aſpirated or pronounced with an h: *Pen*, *Phen*: *Tâd*, *Thâd*, &c.

Further helps to illuſtrate this matter might be derived from the Greek tongue. In that language, letters of the fame organ of ſpeech are frequently changed into one another. The formation of Greek verbs is in a great meaſure founded on this principle; and their characteriſticks are varied in a manner, not unſimilar to theſe mutations of Britiſh conſonants. This, like the former illuſtration, will appear more evident by a table, repreſenting the correſponding changes in each language. I ſhall here retain the examples of the preceding ſcheme, and place, directly underneath each word, the reſembling parts of Greek verbs, and ſhall leave blanks, where there are no correſponding changes.

Câr	Gâr	Nghâr	Châr
Πλι-κω	πιπλι-γμαι		πιπλι-χα
Pen	Ben	Mhen	Phen
κρυ-πτω	ικρυ-βην	κεκρυ-μμαι	κεκρυ-φα
Tâd	Dâd	Nhâd	Thâd
ανυ-τω			ηνυσ-θην
τριχω			θριξω
Bara	Fara	Mara	
λει-βω		λελει-μαι	
Duw	Dduw	Nuw	
αδω			
Gwr	Wr	Ngwr	
λι-γω			
Llaw	Law		
ψα-λλω	ψα-λω		
Mam	Fam		
νε-μω			
Rhâd	Râd		
σπει-ρω			

The above scheme exhibits several variations of letters in each language, formed alike, and upon the same principle. The Greek part indeed does not appear half as full as the British. One reason of that seems to proceed from a deficiency

deficiency in the Greek alphabet; which has a fmaller number of fimple founds than the Welfh: no *ng*, or feparate *h*, among it's palatines; no *f*, i. e. *v*, among it's labials; nor the found of *dd* among it's dentals, or linguals. For this caufe, no changes in that tongue can correfpond with *Fam* or *Fara*, with *Dduw* or with *Nghâr*.

Blanks in the Greek part of the preceding table, may alfo partly fpring from another quarter. Transformations of letters in that tongue are not quite uniform, but frequently depart from the natural order. Only the two firft conjugations feem to be perfectly regular. No others keep to letters of the fame organ. T, δ, ϛ, &c. characterifticks of the third and other conjugations, do not, like the Welfh, change within their own clafs; but take up with preterites, from the palatines or labials, confonants of a different tribe and order from their own. So fond is that tongue of letters of thefe claffes, that no others appear in any

of

of it's preterites, except it may be a *delta* or *theta*, which, by contraction, or some other extraordinary method, become characteristicks of a few preterites in the middle voice.

To illustrate this subject yet further, recourse might be had to the oriental languages. In the Hebrew alphabet are six mutable consonants, called *Litteræ Begadkephat*, having each of them a double sound; one soft and the other hard. For instance, פרו, signifying *fruit*, is founded in different positions, *Pri* or *Phri*, with just the same variation as *Pen* and *Phen*, in the preceding tables. In the same manner, תורה, the Hebrew word for *Law*, is pronounced *Torah* or *Thorah*, like the British *Tâd* and *Thâd*. And so is בנ, a *son*, like *Bara* and *Fara*, founded sometimes *Ben*, and at other times *Fen*, or rather, *Ven*. But these mutations are much more limited in this language, than they are in the Welsh; changeable letters in Hebrew are only six; whereas in the British they are nine: in the

the Hebrew alfo, the change of thefe letters is only double; whereas here they affume three or four different forms.

THE *ufe* as well as the nature of thefe mutations fhould be confidered. They are of very general and extenfive application. By dividing the firft table into declenfions and cafes, it's learned author did not mean to reftrain the ufe of them to nouns and participles, or to fuch words as are the fole objects of declenfions in Latin or Greek. Nor is it intended by comparing them in the fecond fcheme to the characterifticks of verbs, to limit their ufage to fuch words as are the particular fubjects of conjugations. They are of ftill more extenfive application and utility; being applicable to nouns, to verbs, and to words of every other part of fpeech.

In general, they feem to have a twofold tendency; one, refpecting the found; the other, respecting the signification of words.

The first and most obvious use of them is to distinguish the sound, to ease the pronunciation, and to render it smooth and harmonious. Two or more letters of the same organ and of the same sound joined together in a word are lost in pronunciation; they may harden or strengthen a sound; but if they are ever so many they can do no more, and must remain idle and indistinct. Some letters will not be sociable and succeed others; or if they must follow, they will do it with reluctance and difficulty, and give a harsh and discordant sound;—vary these letters, and dispose of them otherwise, and you will put an end to this disagreeable jarring, and make them concur in promoting a general sweetness and melody. For these purposes these changes are often introduced; no other reason need, no other reason can be assigned for several of them.

But

But their chief and principal ufe is to diftinguifh words, to fhow their various relations and connections, and to fix and afcertain their proper meaning. That is the ufe of declenfions, of conjugations, and of other inflections of words in every language, and that feems to be the moft important ufe of thefe changes of confonants in the Britifh tongue. After a manner peculiar to themfelves, they point out the number, gender, &c. not of the fubftantive, for example, where the change happens, but of a pronoun, of an adjective, or of fome other word belonging to it; they form a main part of the fyntax or conftruction of this language; and often contribute to render it's words more diftinct and emphatical.

I would fain hope what has been faid may have brought the reader to be in fome meafure acquainted with this fubject. If it has not proved fufficient for this end, I defpair of being able to afford him that fatisfaction, if it be a satisfaction, and shall forbear giving him any further trouble this way.

WHATEVER it may have proved to the reader, it was a subject of importance to those who were concerned in the publications of the Welsh Bible, and they seem in general to have understood it well. The author of the first table had a considerable hand in the last translation of that book; and the principal conductors of most of it's impressions have taken much pains to render their respective editions exact and accurate in this respect.

Too little attention however was shown to this subject in the earliest impression of the New Testament. We find there *fy garedigion*, *ym plith*, and *yn ty fy tâd*, in the first declension, instead of *fy ngharedigion*, *ym mhlith*, and *yn nhŷ fy nhâd*. And in the second declension we find *fy bara*, *yn Duw*, and *yn golwg*, instead of *fy mara*, *yn Nuw*, and *yngolwg*. It has been since conducted with more regularity

regularity and exactnefs. I cannot but afcribe much of this to the care and accuracy of the very learned Dr. Davies, to whom the language of his country is perhaps more indebted than to any other perfon whatfoever. Some of the earlier impreffions in fome few particulars have yet varied from his plan. They give *fvng byfammod*, Gen. vi. 18. and *fyng hoffadwriaeth*, Exod. iii. 15. which, according to the above fcheme, fhould have been *fy nghyfammod* and *fy nghoffadwriaeth*. Our lateft and beft correctors, I refer particularly to Mr. Morris, and Mr. Williams, have kept more clofely to the plan, and acted more upon the principles of that very able and accurate critick; they have directed their attention not only to initials, but likewife to middle and final letters; and have thus given the language a further degree of eafe and fmoothnefs, rejecting the harfher confonants, and fubftituting others of a fofter found in their place.

In *henw*, *gorchguddio* and *temptio*, they have rejected the h, the g, and the p, and given us *enw*, *gorchuddio*, and *temtio*. For *afcwrn*, *yfpryd*, *datcuddiad*, and *ynthi*, they have printed *afgwrn*, *yfbryd*, *dadguddiad*, and *ynddi*; turning the c, p, t, and th, into the fofter founds of g, b, d, and dd. In the end of words, they have changed *dec* into *dêg*, *oblegit* into *oblegid*, &c. according to the real fpirit and genius of the language; which for the moft part prefers the fmoother and fofter founds to fuch as are more fharp and harfh.

I cannot but approve, and upon the whole commend the general management of this affair. I heartily concur in maintaining the utility and neceffity of moft of the above changes; and if I call in queftion the propriety of any of them, it fhall be done with a temper and conduct, entirely confiftent with a due refpect for thofe who are of a different opinion.

My firft difficulty refpects the number

ber of mutables in Dr. Davies's table. I wifh the lift had been otherwife fettled, and that the r in particular had never been admitted. It feems to have very little right to the character of a mutable confonant. There is a fenfible difference between the found of the c and g, and of all the other examples, produced as inftances of this variation; but between the pronunciation of rh and of the fimple r, or between the found of *rhâd* and *râd*, there does not feem to be any material difference.

Strike out the r, and the third declenfion will appear fimple and plain, and ftand clear of every difficulty; but fo much cannot be faid of the other two.

The fecond declenfion is more fimple than the firft, and attended with the leaft difficulty. It labours however under one miftake, and may be liable to fome other objections. Words beginning with a g are reprefented as turning their radical g into a w in the fecond form;

but this is not accurately reprefented. The g there is not changed into another letter, but is wholly excluded, and the w remains juft where it did; and fo would any other letter, which might happen immediately to follow the g. *Gardd* makes *ardd,* and *glin* makes *lin,* &c. In the other examples of this declenfion, the tranfition from the firft to the fecond ftate appears eafy and natural; but that to the third form is not fo clear and evident; the words feem fomewhat difguifed, further removed from their original ftate, and of more difficult inveftigation.

Thefe objections may be made to the firft declenfion with yet greater force and propriety. From the firft to the fecond ftate, the tranfition is eafy and plain; fo is the tranfition to the fourth cafe; but the change into the third form feems rather difficult and queer. C changes into *ngh,* p into *mh,* and t into *nh;* characters not in the alphabet, and of an awkward make. They are

difpleafing

displeasing to the eye, if not to the ear, and they obscure both the origin and meaning of a word. *Yng nghaer*, *ym mhabell*, and *yn nhŷ*, derived from *caer*, *pabell* and *tŷ*, appear very much disguised, and not easy to be traced home to their proper source.

It may be said, that what is awkward here proceeds from the defect of the alphabet, and it's want of proper characters; that these mutations do not obscure or disguise more than the changes, and probably not near so much as the changes of characteristicks in Greek verbs; and even that, however they may disfigure or disguise, they are yet necessary and unavoidable, and must therefore be endured.

The defect of the alphabet I have acknowledged already; disguise and obscurities arising from the changes of Greek characteristicks must also be admitted; and where such transformations are necessary and unavoidable, I will assent to the continuance of *mh*, *nh*, *ng ng*, and even of *ngh*, the queereſt figure of the whole corps. But I would not bear with them any further; and I could wiſh particularly, with regard to the two laſt, that whenever they come together, one of them might be obliterated, and the other ſuffered to remain alone. But,

Some ſcripture inſtances of theſe changes are not at all neceſſary, and might as well, if not better, have been omitted. *Saith muwch*, Gen. xli. 20. *Pymnŷn*, Gen. xlvii. 2. &c. are of this ſort: variations unnecceſſary and unuſual; and the words are more plain, as well as more common, in another form: *ſaith buwch* and *pymp dŷn*. So alſo 1 Pet. i. 2. *Duw Dâd* exhibits a needleſs mutation, and would have been as plain, and founded better, *Duw y Tâd.*

In other caſes, changes are omitted, where they might, and I think ought, to have been introduced. Gen. i. 8. we read *ail dŷdd*, and ſo uniformly wherever it appears; good judges of
the

the language tell me it is right; but my ear, the cuftom of the country, as far as I can remember it, and the analogy of the language, all affure me that it is not right, and that it ought to have been *ail Ddŷdd.* *Dŷdd* is the abfolute ftate of the word or it's nominative cafe, if I may fo call it; but that is not the ftate which follows the word *ail* in other inftances. We never fay *ail perfon* or *ail gwaith*, but *ail berfon* or *ail waith*; and for the fame reafon, we fhould not fay *ail dŷdd* but *ail ddŷdd*.

One thing more I would juft mention under this article, that in purfuance to this fcheme of changes, and upon the fame principles, the conjunction *ac* fhould, when followed by a vowel, be altered into *ag*; and the initial radical guttural *ch*, if not wholly omitted, might yet be made a mutable, and it's harfh found frequently avoided. There feems to be the more reafon for fo doing, as this letter, I mean the initial

and

and radical ch, is feldom or never pronounced in fome parts of the country. They never fay *chwaer* or *chwerthin*, but *bwaer* or *hwerthin*, throwing away the c and retaining only the h.

It will be faid, thefe are minutiæ,— little matters, and hardly worth notice. I own it, and at the fame time I will fay in return; the eafe, the harmony, the perfpicuity, the elegance, and the fpirit of languages, are frequently much affected by little things; and, if I may be indulged the comparifon, like the peace of families, or even the fate of kingdoms, often depend upon —trifles.

CHAP.

CHAP. II.

NATURE AND PECULIARITIES OF PARTS OF SPEECH IN THE BRITISH TONGUE.

OF letters, the preceding materials, are formed words, the materials again of language, in a fecond and more advanced ftate. Words may be confidered, either with regard to their meaning, or elfe with regard to their make and form; the laft of which, the form of words, is the fubj.ct of this part, by far the moft copious and moft laboured part of grammar.

The moft natural and the moft general divifion of words is, like that of letters, into *mutable* and *immutable*; or, as this has been ufed to be expreffed, into *declinable* and *indeclinable*. This diftinction is rather flighted by Englifh grammarians, as not applicable to their language,

language, which, properly fpeaking, has no declenfions. But the idea of declenfions, ftrictly fo called, is not, at leaft ought not to be, the idea here affixed to declinable and indeclinable. The idea is the fame with that of mutable and immutable; and it is applicable to all languages, and conftitutes the firft and moft obvious diftinction of words.

Look into any book, no matter whether the language of it be underftood or not, it is fufficient if it's letters are known, and it's words diftinguifhed from one another; and you will prefently fee fome of it's words every where uniform and alike; of exactly the fame members and magnitude; or confifting of the fame number of fyllables, and of the very fame letters; others you will fee changeable, and differing from themfelves; fometimes fhorter, and fometimes longer; confifting in different places, of different letters, and of more or fewer fyllables.

INDECLINABLE or immutable words, which are alfo the moft fimple, and the leaft numerous, include, according to the moft common grammar, *adverbs, conjunctions, prepofitions,* and *interjections.*

The laft mentioned (oddly enough called interjection) feems the moft natural and inartificial part of fpeech; if it may be called a part of it, and is not rather a peculiar fort of language by itfelf. It's words feem the rudeft and moft imperfect of all words, being nothing more than an *ah* or an *oh*, or fome fuch fudden exclamation. They are invariable to a peculiar degree, being much the fame in all languages, and and in all ages of the world. They are a part of language little affected, even by the general confufion of tongues; and whatever changes may happen to languages in future, this part of them will remain alike and the fame; as long as the feelings, as long as the fighs and groans of the philofopher, and of the favage, or of men in every age,

con-

condition, and country, will remain alike and the fame. This part of man's language, feems little different from that of the animals below him. It is a fimple effort of nature to relieve itfelf in certain cafes. It forms but a very fmall number of words in any dictionary, and is the clafs of which grammarians have had the leaft to fay.

Next to the interjection, the moft fimple, and the leaft artificial of the invariable parts of fpeech, are the conjunction and the prepofition. Thefe confift, generally, of a fingle letter or monofyllable; and, in fome inftances, they may amount to words of two fyllables. As of themfelves they convey no idea or meaning, they therefore never appear alone, but always in company, and in attendance upon fome other words; and they are employed to connect or to feparate thefe; or, like harbingers and ufhers, to go before and introduce them. Both together they conftitute but a fmall part of the words of any language; and
ufually

ufually good grammars are dictionaries here, and contain them all.

The adverb, reputed another indeclinable part of fpeech, is yet not fo fteady and invariable as the former; neither is it as fimple and inartificial, as the conjunction or prepofition. In fome inftances it is fhort and uncomplicated. Δις, *bis* and *twice*; *hic*, *here*, and *yma*, are little, diminutive words, of a fize and appearance fuitable to their condition and fervile character. But in other inftances, adverbs are words of bulk and dignity. They affume, efpecially in Englifh, an air of peculiar importance; appearing fometimes rather bigger and more fubftantial than almoft any other words of the language. *Surprizingly*, *fuperlatively*, and *furreptitioufly*, may ferve as examples of this kind.

In the Britifh tongue, adverbs are of a more humble and more fimple form, and alfo much fewer than in the Englifh. Adverbs of number, in the ftrict and proper fenfe, I think we have not. Thofe

of

of time, of place, and some others, we have, but not in such plenty as in other languages; and their place is supplied by other words or modes of expression, of which in fact, and in all languages, adverbs are only substitutes. Sometimes a substantive and preposition mean just the same as an adverb. To judge the world righteously, is expressed, Acts xvii. 31, by *in righteousness*, in English, and in Welsh by *mewn cyfiawnder*. But more commonly, this is expressed by a preposition and the adjective, without any substantive. Soberly, righteously, and godly, Tit. ii. 12, we render *yn sobr, yn gyfiawn, ac yn dduwiol*; that is, literally, *in sober, in righteous,* and *in godly*; very awkward, I acknowledge, and nonsensical in English; but not at all so in the British where they stand, but full as proper, and as expressive, as soberly, righteously, and godly; or as *at most*, and as *from everlasting to everlasting*, is in English.

MUTABLE

MUTABLE words, or parts of speech, vary even in their division; some distinguishing them into three parts, (o) viz. *Names, Qualities,* and *Affirmations*;—some dividing them into four, (p) *Nouns, Pronouns, Verbs,* and *Participles*;—others into five, (q) *Articles, Pronouns, Substantives, Adjectives,* and *Verbs.* The last seems the most natural, and the most suitable to my fancy and plan; and I shall therefore follow it in what I have further to say on this part of the subject.

Here again the two first are very uncomplicated and few in number. The article is only a y, a single letter, which in some cases takes to itself an r. The pronoun also is very simple, consisting of one or two syllables at most. The personal pronouns are likewise few, and by nature herself limited to three. They are, however, very variable and irregular, perhaps in most languages, and seem to

P   have

(o) Brightland's Grammar.
(p) Lilly's Grammar.   (q) Lowth's Grammar.

have nothing peculiar in the Britiſh tongue, except it be that in each perſon they are rather in greater plenty and more redundant than in the Engliſh, the Latin, or the Greek. From the air which they aſſume, one would often think them of the greateſt conſequence; but their diminutive ſize takes off much of their importance, and their denomination of *pro-nouns* humbles and leſſens them ſtill more; according to which, words of this claſs, like the adverb, are mere ſubſtitutes, and only ſtand in the room of others.

The ſubſtantive, the adjective, and the verb (the three remaining ſorts of words) are by much the moſt important, and the moſt numerous parts of ſpeech. They are the moſt artificial and complicated of any, and liable to a prodigious variety of changes and viciſſitudes. Subſtantives and adjectives are declinable by caſes, numbers, and genders; adjectives appear different alſo according to their different degrees of

com-

comparifon; and verbs vary by their voices, their moods, and their tenfes, and by their numbers and perfons. But I do not mean here to run through the feveral variations of thefe forts of words, any more than I intend to give a complete lift of their number; one of which is the bufinefs of a dictionary, and the other the particular province of a profeffed grammar. I fhall rather take thefe three principal parts of fpeech together, and confider them in two views, equally applicable to them all.

Wherever we find them, they will appear upon examination to be either *fimple* or *compound*; either *derived* or *underived*; either in their original and primitive, or elfe in their varied and improved ftate. Words fimple and underived, or words in their firft and primitive ftate, I look upon as the firft and original words of a language, as the capital ftock with which it fet out at the beginning, or as the prime materials put into it's hands, if I may fo exprefs myfelf, to manufacture

nufacture and improve. The others, the compound and derived, or words in their varied and improved ſtate, I conſider as the acquired ſtock of a language, as the fruits of it's own labour and induſtry, which it has manufactured and prepared for it's own uſe.

Simple and uncompounded ſubſtantives in their nominative caſe and ſingular number; adjectives of like make, in the ſame ſtate, and perhaps of the maſculine gender, and in the poſitive degree; and ſuch verbs in the firſt perſon ſingular of the preſent tenſe, indicative mood, and active voice, give us the *primitives*, or underived words of a language in their firſt ſtate. All inflections and variations from theſe primitives, whether by formation or compoſition, whether by declenſions, conjugations, or compariſons, give us the *derivatives*, and more laboured words of the ſame tongue. Of theſe two claſſes; the firſt, that is, the primitives, are the leaſt in ſize and in number; they are likewiſe
the

the dictionary words, or the roots in every language; the others, the derivatives, are more bulky, and in greater plenty. If we may judge by the proportion between the nominative cafe fingular and other cafes of the fame fubftantive; more efpecially, if we judge by the proportion between the firft perfon of the verb, and the other parts of it; we fhall find the derivatives to be the moft numerous to a prodigious degree. They would fwell to a moft amazing number, and no dictionary could contain a tenth part of them; but a great many of them are fo regular and plain, that they never need, and feldom do appear in any.

In preparing and ufing thefe derivatives confifts the principal difference of languages, and the vaft advantage of fome above others.

The common folution or analyfis of words into fo many, no matter how many parts of fpeech, may be equally applicable to every language under the fun.

fun. The underived and primitive words of feveral tongues may alfo greatly refemble one another, and be nearly the fame, as proceeding from the fame ftock, perhaps from the original language of man. But a moft wide and amazing difference will be found in their derivatives. Some languages, if I may fo fpeak, treat their original ftock like a fpendthrift; or, like the flothful fervant, take no pains to improve it; they ever ufe thefe materials in their firft condition, or in their ftinted and dwarfifh ftate; while others have laboured and manufactured them, compounded and decompounded them, fo as furprifingly to vary, to increafe, and multiply their firft and original quantity.

The Latin and Greek tongues feem to have diftinguifhed themfelves the moft in this refpect. If we examine any compofition in either of thefe languages, grammars and dictionaries excepted, we fhall find but few words

in

in their fimple and primitive ftate; hardly any monofyllables among the fubftantives, adjectives, or verbs; and if they are thus conftituted in their original form, as foon as they pafs from this ftate, they become polyfyllables, words of bulk and fubftance, which look well, and feem to add weight and dignity to a fentence or period.

The Englifh, on the other hand, feems to have done very little this way. With all it's tendency and difpofition to manufactures and improvement, it has neglected the manufacture and improvement of it's own words. It has gone upon the idle, lazy principle of borrowing and importing; and, rather than take the pains to work and labour it's own materials, it has chofen to become debtor to the French, to the Latin, to the Greek, or to any other language which would truft it with terms ready made and at fecond hand. To this day it ufes it's own native words much in their original ftate, or rather,

rather, in a lefs and more diminutive form. Near two thirds, perhaps, of the words of this language, in it's prefent condition, are monofyllables. Exclude from it all foreign derivatives, and then thefe *little, ftinted, dwarfifh* things will appear in a much more difproportionate number. " Whole lines in a large book will be found like a ftring of beads, made up of words, all of one and the fame fize."

It's derivatives, as well as it's primitives, are frequently of this fort. Adjectives admit of no variety, except that of comparifon; and the variations of fubftantives and verbs often add nothing to their fubftance and magnitude. Love, for inftance, is a fubftantive, and only one fyllable in both numbers. Love alfo is a verb, and almoft the fame in every perfon. Change the fingular into the plural, and join ever fo many fubftantives and perfons together, yet the word remains ftill as unimportant and as fimple as ever. Of this

this fact, *man men, tooth teeth, way ways,* and hundreds of others, are sufficient proof. Most of the varieties of cases and comparisons, of tenses and moods, abounding in some other languages, are here answered by little servile words, called helpers. The most substantial, I had almost said, the only substantial, grammatical variation in the whole extent of the English tongue, is the present active participle.

THE Welsh language has in this respect considerably the advantage of the English; and two circumstances in particular have gained it this advantage.

In the first place, it has more varieties and more substantial grammatical derivatives under each of those parts of speech which we are now considering. Substantives singular become plural several ways, and, in some cases, even two syllables may be thus added to a word: as, *dŷn dynion,* man men, *tŷst tyſtion,*

witness

witnefs witneffes, &c. Adjectives take up thefe plural additions, as well as fubftantives: as, *gwyn gwynion*, white; *trwm trymion*, heavy; they have other means of becoming plural befides; they have alfo a variation in their genders; *gwyn gwen*; and they have even what may be called a fourth degree of comparifon, expreffive of equality: as, *glân, glanách, glanaf, glaned*; *clean, cleaner, cleaneft, as clean.* Verbs in general, efpecially in the active voice, vary their perfons and numbers, their tenfes and moods, by diftinct and particular terminations, and have no need of a large troop of petty auxiliaries or fupporters, fuch as *can, may, could, fhould, fhall, will*, &c. &c. without which an Englifh verb cannot ftand, or ftands for nothing: and they have yet further amongft them a fpecies of reciprocal verbs, or verbs tranfitive on themfelves, like the hithpael of the Hebrew.

The fecond circumftance, giving the Welfh an advantage over the Englifh in in this matter, is the greater liberty it has taken to manufacture it's own materials, to compound it's words, and to form a fet of derivatives different from the above; and the fame as have hitherto alone claimed the name of derivatives. Some of thefe are double, treble, and y t more complicated fhoots from fingle ftocks; and they grow and thrive in great plenty on almoft every Britifh part of fpeech; others of them are formed from the concurrence and united efforts of two or three primitives joined together; which, in either cafe, become complete and diftinct words, by adding the particular terminations of verbs, adjectives, or fubftantives. While the Englifh has gone about borrowing of the French, of the Latin, or Greek; the Welfh has been creating and forming words of it's own; and there feems to have been a fpecial tendency in this language thus to increafe and multiply. By this means it has acquired a confiderable fuperiority

in

in this refpect, and is in poffeffion of feveral verbs and other words, to which I know of none correfponding in the Englifh tongue: as, *dyddhâu, hwyrhâu,* &c. &c.

There are derivatives of this fort manufactured in Britain, by it's original inhabitants, which, in my opinion, are not only fuperior to any thing Englifh in the fame way, but at leaft equal to any productions of the fame kind in ancient Rome or Greece. Inftances will be here expected, to make good fuch an affertion. I fhall content myfelf with giving two or three inftead of many. The firft fhall be, what I may call a double derivative from one fingle root; the fecond, a compound, formed from two fubftances; and the other, a derivative, formed from three fingle and diftinct words.

Arglwyddiaeth, and *arglwyddiaethu,* are Bıitifh goods of the firft fort, home made, and derived from *arglwydd.* *Dominium* and *dominor,* from *dominus*; Κυριοτης and Κυριευω,

Κυριευω, from Κυριος, are the corresponding words of Latin and Greek workmanship, in the same way. I would likewise fain add their English correspondents; from the monosyllable *lord*, I can derive *lordship*, a substantive of two syllables; but I can proceed no further; if there is a verb, it is of the same diminutive form with the primitive. Here the industry and inventive genius of the English fails; but the skill and artifice of the British is, at least, equal to that of Rome and Greece.

Again; *croeshoelio* is a British verb, formed by the union of two substantives, *croes* cross, and *hoel* nail. It is expressive of the manner in which the Son of God was put to death; and it expresses it stronger, and more emphatically, than any words used in this case by the English, the Greek, or the Latin. The English word *to crucify*, according to the genius and analogy of the language, may signify, to make or to be made a cross, as well as to die upon it. The Greek term

term ςαυροω, is no more than *ſtaking*, or faſtening to a pole. The Latin *crucifigo*, more expreſſive here than either of the former (as the puniſhment was Roman) yet means no more than faſtening to a croſs, which may be done various ways. But the Welſh determines the manner of it, and conveys the particular and ſtriking idea of fixing to the croſs with nails.

Further: *Cydymgynghorant*, Iſai. xlv. 21. is another Britiſh compound derivative, formed of *cŷd*, *ym*, and *cynghor*, three diſtinct words; two prepoſitions and one ſubſtantive. It conveys an idea in that paſſage, which neither Hebrew, Greek, nor Latin expreſs, without uſing two different words; and to expreſs the ſame idea in Engliſh, no leſs than *five* different and diſtinct words are uſed.

In both the above reſpects, therefore, that is, in the changes and variations of nouns and verbs, and in the more general formation of other derivatives, the

Britiſh

Britifh tongue has greatly the advantage over the Englifh.

I muft however acknowledge, with regard to derivatives of the firft fort, particularly the inflections of verbs; that the Britifh is not fo full and perfect, as the Greek and Latin. Active participles, I think, it has none. *Caredig*, fometimes fo called, is rather an adjective or participle, chiefly fignifying paffively, and never retaining, like a true active participle, the tranfitive nature of the verb. It alfo wants the prefent tenfe in the active voice; and, for the paffive voice, it has but few diftinct tenfes and terminations. Like the Latin and Greek (both of which are here confiderably defective) it fupplies the place of thefe terminations and tenfes, by the paffive participle and the fubftantive verb, ufed with a pronoun, after the particular manner of imperfonals; or elfe it fupplies this deficiency after a manner peculiar to itfelf, by the verb fubftantive put imperfonally, and the other

ther verb put fubftantively, and preceded by a poffeffive pronoun and prepofition: *yr ydys yn fy ngharu,* I am loved, &c.

With regard to the other fet of derivatives, I would fuggeft a few thoughts, and then finifh this article. Words of this clafs are, undoubtedly, the proper fubjects of our regulation and criticifm; much more fo, than the original and primitive words of a language. To object to primitives, is like objecting to natural and conftitutional bodily imperfections. But objecting to derivatives, is objecting to things of our own making; which, if they are wrong, muft be fo, partly through our own fault. But the misfortune is, here are no rules to direct our conduct; or, if there be, they are *leges non fcriptæ*; fuch as have hardly ever appeared in any grammatical code or fyftem of laws. The Englifh never wanted them, and therefore may never have thought of them. But others, efpecially the Greeks, wanted them, and muft have made ufe of fome regulator,

though

though perhaps unknown to themselves as well as to us. They had simple derivatives, beginning their variations with three or four syllables, such as τετυψομαι, τυφθησομαι, &c. prefix to these a preposition of two syllables, and then add a termination of as many more, and their size would become monstrous indeed;—they would be truly *sesquipedalia verba*, almost literally words of a foot and a half long. We have no British words of such prodigious length, but we have such as are long enough; which, upon an increase of termination, are in common discourse contracted by custom in their radical part, and which, in like circumstances, should, in my opinion, be abridged by authors in the same manner.

From *tragywydd,* for instance, we form *tragywyddol*; and again from thence *tragywyddoldeb* ; derivatives, especially the last, seemingly full long for increase and pronunciation; but in fact, as far as I can recollect, they are never pronounced

ced as here written: they are pronounced *tragwyddol* and *tragwyddoldeb*; the firſt y of the radical excluded, and the words themſelves ſhortened one ſyllable. They are then eaſy to pronounce and to manage, and they had beſt always be ſo written.

The like conduct would not perhaps be improper for long ſubſtantives, which take an addition of two ſyllables to become plural; as *gorchymmyn*, which regularly, in the plural is *gorchymmynion*; a word of five ſyllables, but, I believe, always pronounced as if only four, and as if written *gorchmynion*. In theſe caſes a diſtinct character (r) has been recommended for the firſt y; which character was to be a vowel, to be pronounced, and yet, like the Hebrew ſheva, make no ſyllable; but probably, the eaſieſt and more effectual way would be, to exclude it entirely; for we may change the

(r) The character is the laſt in the fourth column of the table of alphabets, in page 171 of theſe ſheets.

the spelling, and accommodate it to common pronunciation, when we have no authority to coin a new letter and make it current.

I have no other regulations at present to wish, with regard to these derivatives; except it be, that such of them as are compounded of two or more words might always retain, as much as possible, the features of each parent; in which respect some of them may be a little deficient, as Gen. ii. 21. *drym-gwsg*, rather *drwm-gwsg*; and likewise that all of them, whether compounded or not, might be formed, as near as may be, to resemble other words of the language in the same part of speech, in order to be more easily governed by the same laws. Thus I would wish *bedyddiwr, rhagrithiwr,* &c. would cast off the i of the penult, and become *bedyddwr, rhagrithwr,* &c. that together with *breuddwydwr, llafurwr,* &c. they might, with more ease and regularity, change into the plural, *bedyddwyr, rhagrithwyr, llafurwyr,* &c.

CHAP. III.

Nature and peculiar construction of sentences in the British tongue.

HITHERTO we have confidered words, as fingle and unconnected; but they are not to be met with in that ftate, except in grammars or dictionaries. In other books they are brought, as I may fay, to one place, difpofed in a particular manner, and joined together by certain bands, according to rule, and in due form of law. To regulate this matter is the bufinefs of fyntax, the third and laft part of grammar.

The firft ufe of fyntax, σύνταξις, perhaps was military; and from marfhalling men, and drawing up an army, was transferred to fignify the difpofing and regulation of words in a fentence.

If

If this account of it's origin be true, the primary idea here will be that of *ranking*, and the firft work of fyntax will be, to fettle the order and precedence of the different parts of fpeech, according as they ftand in competition for place.

Parts of fpeech in appofition, as they are called, that is, two or more words fignifying one and the fame thing, will, in all languages, be confidered as upon a par, and rank and take place indifferently, as may beft fuit their eafe and convenience.

What are called genitive cafes, or words under government, like good and dutiful fubjects, will keep behind, and follow their fuperiors. In Welfh, however, they receive no increafe of bulk, as in the Latin; they want no prepofition to attend them, after the manner of the Englifh; nor do they take off a piece of the preceding word, in imitation of the Hebrew; let them immediately follow their leaders, as *meibion dynion*, and they are as eafily and as certainly understood, as *filii hominum*, fons of men, or בני אדם.

When fubftantives and adjectives become competitors for rank, the Englifh, in general, declare againft the fubftantive, and give precedence to the adjective; as, *wife* men; the Welfh, on the other hand, for the moft part and more naturally, give the firft and chief place to the fubftantive; as, dynion *doethion*, men *wife*.

As to other different and contending parts of fpeech, the Englifh very naturally make the fubftantive and nominative cafe moftly to precede the verb; but in Britifh, as in Latin and Greek, and other languages, this matter is in a great meafure indifferent; the verb again in it's turn, generally goes before what is called the accufative cafe; and other words lead or follow, as the found fhall direct, or as an author pleafes, to whom great latitude is here allowed.

BESIDES

BESIDES ranking, a further and more common idea of fyntax, is concord, which confifts in a certain agreement between the three principal parts of fpeech, fuppofed to be fettled, either by nature herfelf, or elfe by the authoritative decifions and ftatute law of grammarians. This requires fubftantives and adjectives to agree in their refpective variations of number, cafe and gender; it requires the nominative cafe and the verb to agree in number and perfon; and it directs the relative to accord with it's antecedent in number and gender. Thefe are the general rules and laws of concord, and they are fuppofed to be univerfal, and applicable to every language. But there are few laws and ordinances of men, which deferve univerfal obedience; and fewer ftill, which have never been tranfgreffed.

In the Britifh tongue, the firft law of concord is frequently neglected. As in the Hebrew, fo here, plural adjectives, particularly numerals, are connected

nected with their subftantives in the fingular number, as, *dau ddyn*, two *man*; *wyth enaid*, eight *foul*, &c. Not that this difcord, if I may fo call it, is the invariable cuftom of the language; it has three different methods for this purpofe, either of which may be indifferently followed; we fay, *faith merch*, feven *daughter*; *faith merched*, feven *daughters*; or *faith o ferched*, of *daughters* feven. But fo common, and feemingly fo regular, is the firft method, that I could almoft blame the tranflators of the Bible for deviating from this practice in fome inflances which they have given us of a fubftantive plural with a plural adjective, as Exod. ii. 16; where we have *faith merched*, feven *daughters*; which, for my own part, I will acknowledge, I fhould have been better pleafed with, if it had been *faith merch*, that is *feven daughter*. Again, as the plural adjective will fometimes have a fubftantive fingular, fo, on the contrary, a fubftantive plural will not unfrequently

quently put up with an adjective of the singular number; as, *gwŷr mawr*, not mawrion; *arglwyddi caled*, not caledion.

The second law of concord has more regard paid to it in the British tongue. Verbs generally agree as to number, with the nominative case of the substantive; but yet not without several exceptions. When a substantive singular is joined to a plural adjective, in that case the verb will be plural, and agree with the adjective rather than with the substantive; so Gen. xli. 26. *Y faith dywyfen dêg ydynt*, not *fydd, faith mlynedd*; the seven good *ear* are, not *is*, seven *year*. This example is the reverse of another, not uncommon deviation, from the present rule; wherein the verb substantive, and several other verbs in the singular number, are connected with nominative cases in the plural: *Yr oedd taranau*, Exod. xix. 16. *Bydded goleuadau*, Gen. i. 14. that is, there *was* thunders, &c. &c.

So far I can approve, and will take

upon me to juftify the conduct of a bold language, which difdains the controul of grammatical ftatute laws, where the common law of cuftom, it's original and rightful fovereign, has left it free. The language of the fons of fcience and of liberty, in ancient Greece, acted in the fame manner. Neuters plural in that tongue had their verbs generally of the fingular number; and ἐστί τινες, *there is perfons*, is current, is fterling Greek, and to be found in the beft authors. In both languages, this liberty is taken principally with the fubftantive verb and it's cognates, or relatives. Perhaps it would have been beft to have ftopped here, and not have extended this practice to fome inftances, which might be produced: fuch as, *Y llinynnau* a *fyrthiodd*, Pfalm xvi. 6, the lines *is* fallen, rather, undoubtedly, *are* fallen, *a fyrthiafant*.

Cân, di amhlantadwy, nid efgorodd, Ifai. liv. 1. introduced as an example of a nominative cafe in the fecond perfon joined

joined to a verb of the third perſon, is, I think, firſt miſunderſtood, and then, of courſe, wrong placed; it rather belongs to the third rule of concord, or the agreement between the relative and the antecedent.

This rule requires the relative to agree with the antecedent in number and gender; ſome grammarians add, in perſon. The rule itſelf is not very material in this tongue, as the relative is often, Dr. Davies ſays, is moſt frequently ſuppreſſed. (s) In the above paſſage of the prophet, however, the relative *yr hon* is expreſſed in Italicks, as not in the Hebrew. And I had much rather make this relative to be of the third perſon, and, conſequently, the regular nominative caſe to the verb *eſgorodd*, than conſider this relative as in the ſecond perſon, and ſo introduce a ſpecies of concord, or rather diſcord, which the peculiarities of no language ſeem ſufficient

---

(s) Antiq. Ling. Britan. Rudimenta. pag. 171.

cient to vindicate or excufe. In the Englifh, and other tranflations of the above cited paffage, the verb is taken up in the fecond perfon; thou that *didft* not travail with child; but it is not fo in the original; the literal tranflation of that is, thou who *did* not travail, &c. correfponding exactly with the Britifh verfion; and all the irregularity is, a relative, which may be of any perfon, is regularly connected with a verb in the third perfon, and fomewhat irregularly refers to an antecedent in the fecond.

To thefe peculiarities of conftruction in parts of fentences, commonly preceding the verb, might be added others in parts, which ufually follow it. We have no difference of cafes, or final terminations of words; and therefore no government by verbs of accufative, dative, or other cafes, as in Latin or Greek. What is remarkable, and worthy of notice here, is the frequent ufe of of certain prepofitions, particularly of the prepofition *yn*, after feveral verbs in the conftruction of fentences. They twain fhall be one flefh, Matt. xix. 5. according to the 'Greek is, they fhall be *in* one flefh. The fentence, and the form of it's conftruction, is borrowed from Gen. ii. 24. and is a literal tranflation of the Hebrew. A conftruction exactly fimilar to this appears in the fame paffage of Genefis in the Welfh; but there it is natural and not borrowed; it is no imitation of the Hebrew, but an original Britifh conftruction, where it is much more familiar, and more common, than in the Hebrew itfelf.

After the verb fubftantive, and other verbs, we introduce the prepofition *yn*, to precede nouns fubftantive, in cafes where nothing like it appears in the original. Gen. i. 5. *Duw a alwodd y goleuni* yn *ddŷdd, a'r tywyllwch a alwodd efe* yn *nôs* ; God called the light *in* day, and the darknefs he called *in* night, &c.

Yn

Yn is alfo frequently ufed like the εν of the Greeks, before the infinitive mood, without any pattern for it in the Hebrew: Gen. i. 6. *Bydded y ffurfafen* yn *gwahanu rhwng y dyfroedd*; let the firmament be *in* divide, or dividing, between the waters, &c. And further, without any precedent from the Hebrew, the Greek, or perhaps any other language, it is very often introduced before adjectives alone : Gen. ii. 25. *Yr oeddynt ill dau* yn *noethion* ; and they were both *in* naked, &c. Thefe inftances of conftruction muft feem ftrange, efpecially to perfons not much acquainted with languages; but fuch as are converfant in thefe matters well know, that the peculiarities of all languages appear awkward when literally tranflated into others, but are neverthelefs effential and neceffary to themfelves, and the omiffion of them conftitutes a fpecies of falfe fyntax : witnefs, *edrych wyneb-pryd*, James i. 23. in the Welfh Bible ; which in my opinion is an inftance of wrong conftruction

ftruction, and fhould have been *edrych ar wyneb-pryd.* But,

FURTHER to enlarge on thefe particulars would carry me beyond my plan. What has been faid may be fufficient to give fome idea of the nature, and peculiarities of the Britifh tongue, and of their effect on the ftile and language of the Welfh Bible, which was the profeffed intention of this fecond part.

Of kin to thefe, are two other circumftances of fome influence, which I fhall therefore briefly mention, before I put a period to thefe remarks. One is, the particular circumftance of dialect; and the fecond is, the general nature of Britifh compofitions, previous to the verfion of the Bible into Welfh. Among the Latins, Livy is faid to have his *Patavinity*; and Xenophon among the Greeks, to be both *attick* and *homerick*; and not only thefe writers, but every author will difcover in his compofitions, both the particular dialect of

his

his native place, and alfo the general caft and courfe of his reading.

The perfons concerned in the Welfh verfions and impreffions of the Bible, have been, for the moft part, inhabitants or natives of North Wales. The language of that part of the principality differs in fome refpects from the language of the South. It forms a particular dialect; and fomething of this dialect feems to have been introduced by our tranflators into their verfions. *Yrwan*, for *yr awr hon*, 1 Pet. i. 8, of the firft tranflation; *twymn* and *twymno*, for *twym* and *twymo*, in many places of the prefent verfion; and fome others in every verfion, are of this kind, and after the manner of North Wales.

The fecond circumftance muft have been ftill more operative and influential. Printed books in the Welfh tongue, as I have obferved already, are moftly of a date fubfequent to the Britifh tranflation of Scripture, and therefore cannot be fuppofed to have had here any great

great effect. But there were manufcript compofitions among the Britons prior to that era; and thefe were principally poetical, the works of their much favoured and very venerable Bards. As by the perufal of thefe, I fuppofe our tranflators to have formed their ftile, and fixed, what I may call, their particular manner; fomething of this fort muft not only appear in their tranflation, but alfo in the fubfequent turn, and in the general character of the language fince. Hence, perhaps, feveral of the peculiarities already mentioned; and, it may be, fome others not reducible to any particular clafs. Hence I would derive *gwypont*, for *gwybyddont*; *pum-nŷn* for *pump-dŷn*; *oni ddelo*, for *hyd oni ddelo*; and, *mae Abel*, for *pa le y mae Abel dy frawd*, &c. Thefe words and fentences look like the expreffions of Poets; they are contracted, and deficient in their make or conftruction; and feem as if diminifhed on purpofe to make them anfwer the particular nature and meafure of poetick compofitions.

There are some other words and modes of expression, of which I should have been glad to have given an account: such as *ffun* for spirit, *herlod* for a lad, *gofwyo* for to visit, &c. But, I will freely acknowledge, I have not acquaintance enough with the language to determine, whether they are poetical terms, or whether they are words of a particular dialect in present use, or else, such as were once familiar and common, but are now antiquated. I will, therefore, here finish these remarks, and refer to some abler hand the continuance of what has been overlooked and omitted, as well as the correction of whatever has been said amiss.

CONCLUSION.

IN the preceding obfervations, I have attempted to give fuch as are converfant with languages, and ftrangers to the Britifh, fome idea of it's nature and peculiarities. A more intimate acquaintance, and a further ftudy of this fubject, I would fain recommend to my countrymen, particularly to thofe among them who are perfons of leifure and learning; and I would venture to enfure them, in that cafe, both profit and pleafure.

Their mother tongue was very probably once the moft general and extenfive of any in Europe. In a long courfe of many ages, it may have been affected by fome intermixtures from other languages; but it yet retains more of it's ancient character, more of it's original independence and purity, than perhaps any other tongue in prefent ufe. In it's letters, in it's make, and conftruction, it is artificial and curious to a peculiar degree. In it's different parts and forts of words, it is founding, expreffive, and fubftantial. It has a particular aptitude to vary and to multiply; and, from a few fimple primitives, to branch out and to form derivatives of good mein, of eafy and ftrong fignification, and in great plenty. And in it's difpofition and conftruction of words in a fentence, it has a liberty and variety unknown to many others. This character of it is founded on it's ftate in a tranflation, where it muft have laboured under confiderable difficulties; an original compofition by the authors of that tranflation, would very probably have fet it off to greater advantage. Yet, even thus examined and confidered, it appears highly deferving the attention and ftudy, particularly of the inhabitants of the principality.

This fubject may deferve their regard, not only as curious, but as capable of
throwing

throwing light on some particulars of the history and antiquities of this country. I will take the liberty to suggest one instance or inference of this kind; and then grant the reader his full and final discharge. From the genius and character of the language, therefore, I would infer the state and character of the more ancient inhabitants of Britain.

Their language was artificial, was laboured, and in a more advanced degree of improvement. I cannot help looking upon it as a most venerable, as a most ancient monument of British genius and of British art; more ancient and more indubitable, than their coins or their castles; and more truly and more peculiarly Welsh, than even their mountains. The original, the plain, and the simple language of primitives, may have been the immediate gift and donation of Heaven; the bold and figurative language of tropes and metaphors, may be the effect of the genius

and

and fire of Indians or Savages; but the regular, the laboured language of derivatives looks like the effect of the ſkill and induſtry of thoſe who uſe them. Had we no other monument of Grecian hiſtory and art than the mechaniſm, if I may ſo call it, or than the laboured and artificial character of their language, that alone would be deemed a ſufficient evidence of their being a knowing and improved people. From the ſame conſideration, I ſee no reaſon why we ſhould not draw the like Concluſion, with regard to the former inhabitants of this iſland.

In times paſt they have been repreſented as Barbarians and Savages, as ignorant, and deſtitute of almoſt every improvement and convenience of life; but ſuch a repreſentation ſeems to have been as untrue, as it was unfriendly. The peculiar, the improved character of their tongue, is, to ſay the leaſt of it, a ſtrong preſumption,—that the ancient Celtæ, and, in particular, the ancient inhabitants of Britain, were not in the loweft, but in a more improved ftate of civilization and knowledge. Let Britons of the prefent day, therefore, ftudy and be well acquainted with this moft ancient and moft undoubted monument of the art and fkill of their anceftors. Should fuch a conduct be in any meafure the effect of thefe remarks, I fhall think myfelf happy in having prepared them; and look upon every attending trouble as abundantly compenfated.

FINIS.

AN ESSAY,

ON

THE ANCIENT & PRESENT STATE,

OF THE

Welsh Language:

WITH

PARTICULAR REFERENCE TO ITS DIALECTS.

BEING THE SUBJECT PROPOSED

BY THE

CAMBRIAN SOCIETY,

For the Year 1822.

BY JOHN HUGHES,

Author of *Horæ Britannicæ.*

LONDON:

SOLD BY SIMPKIN AND MARSHALL, STATIONER'S COURT, AND E. WILLIAMS, 11 STRAND; AND BY MR. KAYE, LIVERPOOL; MR. WILLIAMS, BRECON; EVANS AND HARRIS, CAERMARTHEN, AND OTHER BOOKSELLERS.

Priscilla Hughes, Printer, Struet, Brecon.

TO THE

REV. RICHARD DAVIES, A. M.

ARCHDEACON OF BRECON, &c.

A VICE-PRESIDENT OF THE CAMBRIAN SOCIETY

IN GWENT:

THIS ESSAY

ON THE WELSH LANGUAGE,

PRINTED AT HIS EXPENCE,

IS RESPECTFULLY INSCRIBED

BY THE AUTHOR.

PREFACE.

The Essay which is here presented to the Public from the press, has undergone a careful revision, as well as considerable enlargement, since it was put into the hands of the Judges, who decided upon its claims to the distinction conferred upon the Author at the *Eisteddvod*, held at Brecon in the last Autumn. The good opinion then entertained of this production will not, it is hoped, be lessened, at its appearance in print.

The matter comprised in the Appendix, is in addition to the original paper presented to the Cambrian Society; entirely so, with the exception of a part of the poetical Extracts. The whole taken together will, it is presumed, not prove an uninteresting accession to the Essay itself.

To those who are but slightly versed in the Welsh language, it will be pleasing to find, that our poetic treasures are so richly varied and so copious. The Prose Extracts ought, perhaps, to have been larger, to please the curious; but the translations subjoined prevented further augmentation. The judicious Cambrian cannot avoid lamenting, that our ancient Prose writers fall so far short in their departments of the excellence of our Bards; though in the Triads, we meet with a succinct neatness and terseness of expression, in many instances, highly creditable to our Ancestors.

In the Remarks on the Welsh Orthography and Composition, it need only be said here, that while the Author of the Essay is aware, there are respectable men of sentiments opposite to him, he is well assured, that those on his own side, are equally respectable.

The reader is to be apprised, that as the precise object of the Essay more particularly regards the state of the Welsh language in the present day, with an especial regard to its dialects, he has declined entering deeply into the question of its antiquity, that having already been so ably done in several productions of recent date.

In the present endeavour to investigate our ancient mother-tongue, the reader will find no hostility to the English language; for he is equally averse to narrow-minded bigotry and local prejudices, as to want of attention to the Welsh language, where it should be cultivated. As to those who are still disposed to treat the language with contempt; let them be advised, to inform themselves a little on the subject, and they may possibly abate in their opposition, as their information increases. Let them at least give credit to the promoters of the Cambrian Societies, for having no object in view, inconsistent with either the literary improvement or public welfare of their native country; being well persuaded that it is the duty of every respectable Cambrian, to excite the mental energies and elicit the dormant talents of our countrymen. With such a design, the Author of the piece now before the public, could not decline coming forward in a cause, worthy of greater abilities than he is possessed of.

For further illustration of various topicks touched upon here, as well as the general object, the reader is referred to Mr. Owen's excellent Grammar in English, and Mr. Robert Davies's, composed in Welsh; or to those who approve of the old Orthography, Richards's Grammar is recommended, and which may be had in a portable form and size. The Rev. Mr. Walter's Dissertation, and Mr. Humphreys Parry's Essay on the Welsh language should be here noticed, as well as several papers in the Cambrian Register. In the Celtic Researches and Horæ Britannicæ, information will be found interesting to the Cambrian Antiquary, on the general principles and theory of our language, compared with other ancient tongues, to which it bears an affinity; but the study of Mr. Edward Lhuyd's Archæologia Britannica, is particularly recommended to the general student in philology, as comprising a treasury of Celtic literature.

It was designed here to give a concise sketch of Welsh grammar, particularly as to the plural terminations of nouns, and the formation of the verb in its moods and tenses; but I shall only make a few remarks, which may prove of use to some readers.

The plural terminations are various, either by augmentation as *dyn, dynion; bryn, bryniau; mor, moroedd,* &c.; or by adding only the letter *i,* as *rhes, rhesi.* Some nouns form the plural by a change of the vowels, as *march; meirch; sarph, seirph; castell, cestyll;* others again both change and augment, as *gwas, gweision; dall, deillion; bwrdd, byrddau.*

The nouns of number seem to be derived from the Latin and Greek, like those in English and French; *un, dau, tri, pedwár, pump, chwech, saith, wyth, naw, deg,* &c. The Welsh adjectives have the plural number in most instances, and generally follow the noun as in Latin and Greek: and have the distinction of gender.

The root of the verb is the infinitive, or more properly the imperative, which accords with the views of some of our modern linguists, and is a theory most simple and rational, and founded in nature.

The present tense is either formed by the use of the auxiliary, or the future form, as in *credu*, believe:

Wyf yn credu, I do believe, or I am believing.
Credaf yn Nuw, I believe, or I'll believe in God.
Credwn is the imperfect tense;
Credais is the perfect tense;
Credaswn is the preterperfect;
Crêd is the imperative mood.

The passive voice is not much in use in Welsh, and has a good deal of the impersonal form, thus: *Rhoddir*, in the present; imperf. *Rhoddwyd*, without variation in all the persons and in both numbers, which is the reverse of the active, as for instance in the perfect tense: *credais, credaist, credodd*: pl. *credasom, credasoch, credasant*. The potential, optative and subjunctive moods, are expressed by auxiliaries.

The instances of dialect which are given, will admit of considerable amplification, both as to the use of words, and the variety of the terminations. Many things of that kind will occur to the intelligent reader, who is acquainted with various parts of the Principality. The following are a few additional instances.

South Wales. *Diogel,* as *ffordd ddiogel; rhwtto* for *rwbio; chwalu* for *chwedleua; prudd,* as *gweddio yn brudd; cwnnu* for *codi; stwr* for *swn; mysgu* for *dattod;* the word *cettyn* for *darn; corwybr* for *llwytrew; ffel* for *têg* or *glân; prydferth* for *llonydd; cadnaw,* a fox.

Many words used in the counties of Cardigan, Pembroke and Merioneth, might be collected: as to the Silurian dialect, all who are versed in our ancient writings, may observe its peculiarities; some of which in respect to terminations in particular, may arise from the affectation of writers, as *bracheido,* &c.; but it contains many fine words and neat idioms. Almost all our old prose writings come from Siluria, having been preserved there, either by the industry of the Bards, or of the Monks of Llancarvan.

The Author here begs leave to express his respectful acknowledgments to the Rev. W. J. Rees, for his friendly and prompt communications, and at the same time to return similar thanks to the Rev. Walter Davies. After the perusal of the criticisms of the latter gentleman, the following notes were drawn up.

In p. 16, the letter *w* is regarded as a consonant, that is more particularly in the beginning of words, as in *wiw, weuau,* &c. though in the beautiful lines there inserted, some would say there is no consonant; but we are willing to stand corrected by the Critics, only offering the following remarks:—In the words *gwin, gwynt, gwellt, gwych,* &c. (where the sound of *w* differs much from the same in *hwnt* and in *hwythau*), it has *the force of a consonant,* (consonæ vim obtinet) as Dr. Rhys observes. The Breton Grammarians use the dipthong *ou,* agreeable to the French mode, where the Welsh use *w,* as in *chouech* for *chwech;* so the

Greek *oinon,* answers to the Latin *vinum,* the English word *wine,* and the Welsh *gwin:* a curious instance of variation of sound.

In the scheme of sounds given in p. 18, 19, Mr. Walters is chiefly followed, and it is presumed to be sufficiently accurate, to afford strangers a notion of the genius of the Welsh language, as to the power of the letters. But the Critics may object that the sound of the Welsh *u,* is not exemplified in *green,* or in *meet, street;* or the two-fold sound of the *y,* occurring in *hynny,* clearly illustrated by the English word *sundry.* That twofold sound ought more accurately to be noted by two distinct characters, as in Dr. Rhys and Dr. Davies.

With regard to the instances given of different words used for the same thing, or the various aacceptation of the same word, generally either in North or South Wales; the usage referred to, may not in every instance specified extend, through all the Counties of either Province; and within the same County there may be a difference, in the use of words, or the meaning affixed to them. It may also happen, that the words ascribed to South Wales, either as to the entire or the frequent use of them, may be in use in the contiguous parts of North Wales, as for instance in Montgomeryshire. On the other hand, in parts of Cardiganshire, an approach to the dialect of the North may be observed, and this may arise a good deal from that intercommunity, which several causes have recently conduced to facilitate. But the variations and distinctions marked out in the Essay, have an actual existence, although there may be some mistakes as to the limits of country alluded to; but in general the Author deems himself correct, from the actual observations he has had occasion to make.

The instances given in the general Table would admit of a nicer classification, and with the use of asterisks and obelisks, the distinctions might have been carried to a greater exactness. But whatever defects capable judges may discern, they will allow, as a respectable correspondent intimates, that a good deal has been done which may hereafter lead to further improvements.

Let not then the first thing of the kind offered to the public, be too rigidly scanned. From the exercise of fair and candid criticism the author does not shrink.

The extracts given from various productions, will serve to shew the difference of orthography, as well as of the style and language in different ages, and authors of different tastes. In the observations offered, and the suggestions given, the author has no other aim than the good of his countrymen, and the extension of useful knowledge among them. The style as well as the orthography of the Welsh Bible, he is fully of opinion, is the proper standard for the language; and he feels much for his worthy countrymen, that they should be so perplexed by continual innovations. The rejection of the double letters, where the etymology does not strictly require it, may appear plausible; and if these be rejected only in the plurals of nouns and the terminations of verbs, the objection would not be so great, but it must be mere affectation to write, *eto, hyny*, for *etto* and *hynny*. The new plan is also objectionable as it is injurious to the euphony of the sound, when we have *anmarch, yn mhellach*, for *ammarch* and *ym mhellach*. As to variety in the terminations, we do not object to the poetic license, or to certain ingenious efforts in prose; but the honest Welsh yeoman, among his native hills, looks best in a good plain suit: neatness will add to his respectability, but frippery only exposes him to derision.

Errors of the Press, &c.

Page 8, l. 20, *for* nice, *read* nicer.
 15, l. 17, *read* Tàn a dwr, &c. l. 23, Nwthyn, mwthyn.
 16, l. 4, *for* ym mhola, *read* ym mola.
 20, the mutable consonants are, c, p. t; b, d, g; ll, m, rh.
 23, l. 6, *for* confers, *read* confer.
 25, l. 11, *for* appears, *read* appear.
 30, l. 18, add—In South Wales, *di* at the beginning of some words is changed into *g*; as dioddef into goddef, dywedyd, gwedyd: *f*, is often quiescent, as cofl, còl.
 32, l. 2, *read*, has. Do. l. 24, *read*, houl, dou.
 33, l. 21, *add*, mor, *as* mor laned.
 34, l. 15, *for* arloes, *read* arllwys.
 40, l. 12, at the end, *read*, and.
 Do. l. 18, *for* esmyth, *read* esmwyth.
 61, last but one, *read*, for Romans, Normans.
 79, l. 12, yn ysgafn hefyd. l. 14, gwrthddrych.
 94, l. 3, *read*, gadwynog.
 96, l. 23, *read*, Saeson clawdd y cnwccin.
 99, l. 5, *for* brydydd, *read* bardd.

AN ESSAY,

&c.

The ancient language of Britain, as still preserved in the principality of Wales, is entitled even to the notice of those who are strangers to the country where it is in use, while it particularly claims the regard of the Cambrian. The history of a language, is intimately blended with that of the people who speak it; and when the one falls into neglect, the other sinks into a state of barbarism. A due regard to the honour and credit of our country, should induce us therefore to enter upon the inquiry now before us.

The natives of Wales, as the only badge of their ancient independence, claim the right of retaining in a cultivated form, the dialect once used by the heroes of ancient

Britain, by her Bards, her Sages, and her Divines. This right is neither claimed nor conceded to its full extent, even in matters of great civic interest, such as the administration of the law; but in religion, it is conceded by the authorized version of the Sacred Volume, and Formularies of the Church.

There are many in the principality, who are not under an immediate necessity of having recourse to the Welsh language; but even such persons may feel an interest, as a matter of curiosity, in the topics to be treated of in the present Essay; and to such it is in a great measure addressed. To the scholar we may venture to affirm, that the Welsh is the best preserved of all the ancient dialects of this part of the world, and contains literary stores extremely curious; affording to the Antiquary those important helps, the want of consulting which, has caused many celebrated writers to fall into palpable errors.

The plan of the present attempt is; To inquire into the history of the Welsh language at various periods:—To take a survey of its structure and its properties, and more particularly of its dialects:—To notice its present state, and the best policy to be pursued in reference to it.

I.—As to the history of our ancient tongue, we shall not professedly take upon us the task, though by no means an unpleasant one, to trace its remote antiquity. That has already been done so ably and so successfully, that we shall not enlarge on that head. The structure of the Cymraeg, evinces its affinity with languages which confessedly are regarded the most ancient, and particularly the Hebrew; as to which a learned Antiquary has affirmed, "That the British tongue, having more of that original language in it, than all the rest together, may merit the esteem of being reckoned the *most ancient and least corrupted language in this western part of the world.*"

It will admit of historical evidence, that the natives of Wales are descended from those ancient Britons, who were the original inhabitants of this island, and that they now speak the same language as their forefathers, who opposed the Romans, and afterwards the Saxons.

The ancient Gauls and Britons spoke a language nearly similar, as appears from Cæsar and Tacitus, and other ancient writers; and that there was no mistake committed by those great Romans, is clearly proved by the circumstance, that the Celtic of Britany, and that spoken in Wales, still bear a close affinity to each other.

The Welsh or the Cymraeg, is one principal branch of the great Celtic stock, to which along with the Teutonic, we may trace all the languages of Europe, until important changes were effected by the introduction of Latin. A learned writer, on the origin of the European languages, has divided the Celtic into two branches; the one he styles the Magogian, under which he classes the Irish, and the other the Gomerian or the Welsh. But after that distinction, he has instanced in no less than *a thousand words,* the affinity between the languages of each class(¹).

That the Welsh was anciently spoken on the South-Eastern coast of this island, as well as on the Western, is rather questionable; but that it was spoken on that side from Cornwall to Cumberland, and from the Solway to the Clyde, and perhaps from the Humber to the Forth, we have reason to believe. We may venture further to affirm, that, as it is a plausible supposition, the Pictish dialect was but a slight variation of that spoken by our ancestors, it therefore extended at one time through a great part of Scotland.

The establishment of the Romans in Britain, may reasonably be supposed to have produced a great effect in modifying the language of the natives, as well as inducing many within the municipal towns, to adopt that of their conquerors. Among the Roman Britons there were persons who

---

(¹) See Dr. Parson's Historical Inquiry on the Origin of the European Languages.

cultivated both tongues, as the English and the Welsh are cultivated among us in the present age. There is evidence, that our language is indebted to that of Rome for many of its terms, and probably, for its grammatical forms.

The prevalence of the Saxon arms, became the means of confining the language, within the territorial bounds, which continued to distinguish between the Cymry and the Anglo-Saxons; but the names of several rivers, mountains and ancient stations, out of the confines of Wales, are to be traced to the British tongue. Devonshire and Cornwall long retained it, and in particular the latter county, where a few persons continued to speak it, within the last century[2].

But when the Saxons gained the possession of the territory from the Britons, did they not acquire in some degree at least,

---

[2] See Price's Cornish Grammar, as well as Mr. Llwyd's Archaeologia Britannica. The names of places in Cornwall are nearly all Welsh.

the manners of the people over whom they gained the ascendancy, and blend their language with their own? History as well as Analogy, will warrant a reply in the affirmative. Alfr d borrowed many of his regulations from the ancient Britons, and engaged a Cambrian scholar to lay the foundation of his University at Oxford([3]). The local divisions of the country, and the trial by jury, were taken from the old Britons, and as to language, notwithstanding the difference in the form, several words are radically the same; for one, who was a minute investigator of those matters, tells us, he could discover 3000 words of British origin in the English([4]). In the French, the number of words derived from the Celtic is very considerable.

The Britons of Cornwall, of Wales, and

([3]) Asserius, a learned monk of St. David's, who assisted the royal Legislator in forming his Code of Laws, and constituting those regulations by which he has transmitted his fame to the latest posterity. The grateful Monarch made Asserius, who is called *Bardd Glas* among the Welsh, Bishop of Sherborn.

([4]) Whitaker's History of Manchester, B. II.

of Cumberland, valiantly withstood the aggression of the Anglo-Saxons, but the Welsh alone were able with success to defend their own country, and permanently to retain their own language. We have still extant, the remains of Llywarch and Aneurin, chieftains and warriors of the North; men who bore a name as heroes in their day, and are still revered as ancient Bards, who described the battles in which they were personally engaged, and the calamities which they had to deplore; bereaved of their kindred and their friends and driven from their territories. The Welsh of these Northern chiefs, as well as that of Merddin, is full as intelligible as that of Taliesin; and from their writings we perceive, that the language was copious and cultivated in their day, though their poetry was not subjected to the nice rules of a subsequent age.

For more than four centuries, Bardism appears to have been on the decline, until the flame again broke out under the patronage of Griffith ap Conan in the eleventh century. From that era we find the names of Meilyr, Gwalchmai and Cynddelow, Bards of the first celebrity; there were also Gwynvardd Brycheiniog and Llywarch, who were followed by others until the fall of Llewelyn ap Griffith; a tragical event, which awakened all the plaintive energies of the Bard, and " the deep sorrows of the lyre." The dreadful havoc of that order attributed to the first Edward, we wish for the sake of humanity to discredit, and more especially as clear historic evidence is wanting, to confirm that dismal tale of the olden days.

After the subjugation of Cambria, we shall only take notice of Davydd ap Gwilym, a native of the county of Cardigan, who spent much of his time in the East of Glamorgan, (now included in Monmouthshire), under the patronage of *Ivor Hael*, the lord of Basalic, whose generous descendant at this time presides over the province of Gwent.

We have numerous manuscripts of the Bards of the middle ages, a selection of whose works are published in the Welsh Archaeology, to which an addition it is

c

hoped will be made, by the munificent supporters of the Cambrian Institution. These sons of the Lyre, have not wanted for successors in every age, and in the present day we have ample proof, that the same genius, the same fire, still survives to animate the efforts and to glow in the compositions of our contemporary Bards.

Among the prose compositions of the middle ages, we have the laws of Howel Dha, the Mabinogion or Fairy Tales, collections of moral Aphorisms, the Triads and the Chronicle; with various works, some of which aspire to no great merit of authorship, while others evince considerable acquaintance with the powers of the language. But the Bards are generally regarded, as the grand conservators of the Welsh tongue[5], for they gloried in guarding its purity and keeping it free from admixture with foreign words. Here we may pause, to make an observation flattering to a Cambrian's pride; that while the Monks

---

[5] This requires some qualification, as the poetic style, particularly in Welsh, has certain peculiarities.

were chaunting their orisons in Latin, our Bards were pouring forth their strains in their vermacular tongue, during a period when Europe was sunk in barbarity, and the fathers of English poetry were constructing uncouth rhymes. David ap Gwilym, the Cambrian Petrarch, composed in all the beauties of his native language, in a style that continues to charm; while Gower and Chaucer failed to make the courtly English, the vehicle of any thing, which in a more polished age could be deemed poetry.

The elevation of the Tudors to the English throne, raised the Welsh people from a state of subjugation, to that of a country incorporated with the realm of England. An event so auspicious could not fail to produce a corresponding influence, on the compositions of the Cambrian muse.

Queen Elizabeth, in particular, gave every encouragement to the Bards, and more than one general congress was held under her reign and her auspices.

It was in the days of good Queen Bess, that an undertaking of the highest consequence to the moral interests of the Cambrian was completed, which, like every step, having the same great object in view, has been attended with those results, which prove it to have been founded in just as well as liberal policy. I shall be understood here, to refer to the translation of the Sacred Volume into the Cambro-British tongue, accompanied with the Forms of Divine Worship. Hereby we were saved from barbarism, and were made a Protestant people; and the respect shown to the ancient language of the country, gained the affections of our countrymen, and ensured their loyalty; for the Cambrians will ever be loyal to a paternal government, though they never can submit to be slaves.

A policy the reverse of this, pursued with respect to languages esteemed barbarous by Imperial Rome, brought on that dark night of ignorance and superstition, under which Europe long groaned. The same cause, the neglect of the native language of the community, has been the grand reason why Ireland, fertile and beautiful as is its soil, remains in a state so degraded and so pitiable. How different is the situation of Wales and of Scotland, from that of Ireland and Brittany! In the two former countries, the ancient language of the natives is cultivated, and they appear a civilized, moral and happy people; and it shall be left to others to prove, that the inhabitants of the two other countries are equally civilized and equally happy.

II.—We shall now proceed to take a survey of our native tongue, in reference to its general character, its structure and its properties Here we have strong prejudices to combat, from the ignorant and the learned, who both combine together, to calumniate the old British as an irregular and inharmonious language, unfit to be the vehicle of fine sentiment, and so rugged, as to deter persons of taste from paying regard to it; and this is evident, they exclaim, from the unsightly appearance of its vast number of consonants, and especially the gutturals.

But all this is grounded either on pure mistake, as to the orthographical appearance, or as to certain sounds proceeding from the mouths of the rudest of our peasantry. But that language which is the vehicle of so much fine poetical composition, carefully preserved and handed down from age to age, and in which we continue to have productions that interest and charm us, cannot be so mean and pitiful as its enemies would represent it to be. It is not a mere sorry dialect as they are apt to imagine, incapable of being reduced to the rules of general grammar; nor so confined in its nomenclature, as to possess only a paucity of words and scantiness of expression, rendering it unfit for use on subjects of any extent and importance. It might be supposed, that we have neither Grammar nor Dictionary, whereas we have both drawn up two centuries back, by a scholar of distinguished parts, for such Dr. Davies unquestionably was, to whom we may add Dr. John David Rhys. Since their days we have had the learned and ingenious Edward Llwyd, in the beginning of the last century; and the present age has produced a work which rivals that of Johnson. It will be understood that I refer to

Dr. Owen Pugh's Welsh and English Dictionary, containing upwards of a hundred thousand words. Next to this, if not equal to it in utility, is the laborious English and Welsh Dictionary of that elegant scholar the late Rev. John Walters of Cowbridge, the author also of an admired Dissertation on the Welsh Language. That the Welsh is capable of expressing the most harsh and rugged sounds, we do not attempt to deny, and in this we have a proof of its powers; but let it not be forgotten, that no tongue possesses a finer capacity of expressing soft and delicate sounds. We shall give a specimen of both.

ON THUNDER.

Dŵr a thân yn ymwriaw
Yw'r taranau, dreigiau draw!

Example of a sonorous and vigorous versification in which the liquids *n* and *r* take the lead:

Mae'n bwrw'n Nghwmberwyn, mae'r cysgod yn estyn,
Gwna heno fy pwthyn, yn derfyn dy daith;
Cai fara a chawl erfyn iachusol a chosyn,
A menin o'r enwin ar unwaith.

The following lines on the Harp, are peculiarly soft:

Mae mil o leisiau meluson,
Mae mêl o hyd ym mhola hon.

Within the womb of this are found
The charms of sweet enchanting sound.

The following lines on a Silk-worm have not one consonant except *w*:

O'i wiw wy i weu e â, a'i weuau,
O'i wyau e weua,
E weua ei we aia,
Ai weuau yw ieuau ia.

From his own eggs the busy worm
Attempts his hasty webbs to form,
Like rings in ice, they seem to view,
Beauteous like those and brittle too.

Among the specimens of Welsh poetry given in the Appendix, will be found instances of soft and harmonious verse, equal to what can be produced in any language. Let it not then excite the scoff of the fastidious, when it is affirmed, that men of the first abilities and the finest taste, have shown a strong and marked predilection for the Welsh language; among these we may mention the learned **Edmund Prys,** Archdeacon of Merioneth, who preferred the strains of the Cambrian Muse to those of any other nation and people. His words are:

> Ni phrofais dan ffurfafen
> Gwe mor gaeth ar Gymraeg wen.
>
> *What strains of elegance beneath the sky*
> *Can with the Cambrian muse presume to vie.*

The double letters, used for want of appropriate characters to express the sounds of the language, are certainly an eye-sore, but it should be recollected, how uncouth an appearance the Hebrew and the Greek make in Roman letters. The doubling of the liquid *n* and the frequent use of *h* as an aspirate, may be objected to, but considering the circumstances of most Welsh readers, plainness and utility must be preferred to neatness of appearance. Proposals have been offered to remedy these blemishes, but such as are not likely to meet with the general approbation of the Welsh community; and a few curious persons should not be anxious to please their own taste at the expence of utility([4]).

The common Welsh characters with the appropriate sounds are here subjoined. Those that differ not from the English sounds are not noticed.

Character.   *Pronunciation.*

A,   as *A* English, in *Man*; but when circumflexed, as in *Fare, Mare.*

C,   is always hard like *K.*

Ch, is a guttural, answering to the Hebrew Cheth, and the Greek *X*, which might be used by the Welsh.

Dd, or Dh, as *Th* in the words *Then, That*, &c.

E,   as in *Ten, Fen*, &c. sometimes like the slender sound of the English *A*, or *Ea*, and the French *E.*

F,   as *V* in general, or as *F* in *Of*. *V* is used in many old Welsh MSS.

Ff, as *F* English; or *Ff* in *Off.*

G,   is always hard as in *Gain, Gone*, &c.

I,   never sounds shrill, as in *Fight, Right*,

━━━━━━━━━━━━━━━━━━━━━━━━
([4]) See the Remarks on Orthography in the Appendix.

but similar to the French, or as the English *I* in *Hid, Bid,* &c. and often soft, as *Ee* in *Feed, Deed,* &c. It often ends a word, like *Y*, in *Softly.*

Ll, or Lh, the aspirated *L*, which is the most difficult sound for a stranger to acquire. The Biscayans and the Anglo-Saxons seem to have had it.

O, as *O* English, in *Gone, Honey,* &c. or as in *Bone, Hope, Home.*

Th, the same as in *Think, Thick,* &c.

U, never to be sounded, as in *Muse, Music,* &c. but as more prolonged than the Welsh *I*, like *Ee* in *Green,* or similar to the French *U*, in *Un* or *Une.*

W, 1st, like *Oo* in English, or *Ou*, French, or the *U* circumflexed in *Hindû.*
2d, as a consonant, in *CaerWorgan,* &c.

Y, as *O* in *Word,* or *U* in *Burn;* or as *Y* English at the end of words. Both sounds are expressed in *Sundry,* and in the Welsh words *Hynny, Ystyr.*

In the Welsh alphabet, there is no *J*, nor *Q*, nor *X*, nor *Z;* but they may at times be adopted to express foreign names.

The *J* might be used with the French pronunciation. For *Q*, *CW* is used as in *Cwestiwn*.

In Welsh, every character expresses a definite sound, which never varies, so that when the powers of the letters are acquired, there is no further difficulty.

In order to facilitate pronunciation, and to form grammatical inflexions, there are certain changes of the initial letters, in the Welsh, Breton, and Irish languages.

The *mutable consonants* are *c, p, t, d, g, ll, m, rh:* these are to be formed into *three* classes, with *three letters* in each.

The *principle* of *mutation* is also *threefold;* that is to say, the *light*, the *aspirated* and the *soft* sounds([5]).

CLASS 1. Consisting of *c, p, t,* is susceptible of all the three kinds of modification; as, *cân, ei gân, fy nghân, ei chân.*

([5]) The vowels are also subject to changes.

Class 2. Consisting of *b, d, g,* has two modifications; as, *buwch, ei vuwch, fy muwch.*

Class 3. Consisting of *ll, m, rh,* has but one modification; as, *llaw, ei law.*

The Welsh language is not deficient of any of the properties, which are considered essential to a good language, especially if we make some allowance for the limited sphere of its operations, and the disadvantages to which they who speak it, are subject. It possesses copiousness of primitives, great number of derivatives, and has the power of forming compounds, with the utmost facility. The grammatical forms are regular, though not complex; the terminations of its nouns are various and yet definite; and the inflexions of the verbs are well arranged. The general principles of concord are precisely defined, and it is suited for either the plain or the florid style. It comprises a variety of sounds, which by proper combination, renders it harmonious; for while it is sonorous and guttural, it abounds with sounds the most soft and delicate; it can descend to subjects little and familiar, or rise to those that are the most lofty and elevated. In these respects, it is like the country where it is used, and which abounds with mountainous heights, stupendous precipices, and roaring cataracts ; but there are the sloping hills, the rivulets murmuring through the glade, the fields waving with corn, and the fertile pastures.

The Bards know how to adapt those qualities of their language, in the most skilful manner, in the constructing of their verse; so as to form an unrivalled species of poetry, by a proper combination of vowels and consonants. Its powers of expression in the hands of a master are grand and mellifluous, yielding to none in that property, which renders the sound an echo to the sense. As evidence of this, the reader is referred to the selections given in the Appendix. If we turn to the first chapter in the Bible, or to the sublimest passages of the Psalms or the Prophets, to the Decalogue or the Paternoster; the Welsh version appears under no disparagement in contrast with the English. It has been often remarked, that the liturgy in Welsh, has a peculiar pathos and grandeur.

The mutations of the initial letters, partly by way of grammatical inflexions, and partly by assisting the euphony of pronunciation, confers great beauty on Welsh composition. Without this property, in connection with the rules of just metre and consonancy, its poetry would in truth, be rugged and dissonant in some instances, and exceeding weak and feeble in others; whereas by due attention to the regulations adopted, the efforts of the Cambrian Muse are flowing and harmonious, as well as vigorous.

As to the gutturals of the Welsh, those are found in most ancient languages, and in several of the modern. By rejecting them, etymology would be lost, and the vigorous tone of a noble language greatly diminished. The Anglo-Saxon, the parent of the modern English, is not destitute of them, and the German, which is allowed to be an excellent language, has them. But a good deal depends on the pronuntiation, so that without destroying the force of expression, words and sentences appearing harsh in the mouths of some speakers, would produce a different effect, with a proper modulation. It would be thus, were the language more generally cherished by the higher classes.

The common dialect, spoken by the peasants of Wales in general, is not a fair criterion, by which to judge of the merits of the Welsh language. It would be equally fair for foreigners to form a judgment of English, from the colloquial jargon of the common people in various parts of the kingdom. The capacity, information and manners of the peasantry differ, in various parts of Wales, as well as of England, and the former in many instances are not inferior to the latter; but there is a standard, to which the generality pay no great attention. Good writing is the standard of language, but as there is a corrupt mode of speaking, so there is a corrupt mode and habit of writing; both the one and the other may arise, either from rusticity and negligence, or from erroneous instruction. That the language should be both spoken and written, too frequently in a corrupt manner, need not surprize us; but that many of our peasantry speak their native tongue with so great purity and correctness, is a circumstance creditable to the country.

III.—That striking variations are to be observed in the language, as generally spoken in different parts of the principality, is sufficiently evident; and these at first appear very formidable, when persons from opposite districts meet with each other. This particularly affects the pronunciation, which forms the greatest difficulty in conversation; for the Welsh, as a written language, does not comprise so many variations as in its colloquial forms. Here we must also distinguish between mere negligence, and that which generally causes one district to vary from another, and claims some attention among grammarians. There may be a little difficulty here, in forming a general standard. In a national language the difficulty is less, but it is different with respect to a people, whose language is not now used, nor in the court, nor in the senate; and whatever it was at one time, is now no more than a provincial tongue. The Greek had its dialects, and these we may observe in the writings of Herodotus and Thucidides, of Homer and Theocritus.

In the great writers of Rome, we perceive no variations of dialect, for the Imperial city gave the standard to all the eminent writers, and no variation was admitted; but in modern times, Rome, Milan and Florence have distinct dialects of the Italian. The English language, like that of ancient Rome, knows no dialects, but what is considered as arising from corrupt and rustic habits.

Disputes, it is true, might be set up, and it would be difficult upon any general theory to come to a decision on certain points of discussion. Why might not the broad Scotch, and the dialects of Yorkshire and Lancashire, put in their claim for consideration, to stand in the same relation to the English, as the Dorick to the Greek language; and why should not the natives of London insist upon *their peculiarities* as

Attic English? In the north of England, certain words are softened in pronunciation, and probably are a nearer approach to the genuine modulation of the language; but this plea will not avail, for our great authors and lexicographers, and the usage of polished life, form the standard from which we are not allowed to dissent.

According to the ancients, there are three dialects:—that of North Wales; that of South Wales in general, and in particular Demetia or Dyved; and the Silurian, commonly called Iaith Morganwg, and at other times Iaith Gwent and Iaith Syllwg. With respect to these different usages, there are some things to be rejected in every one; although in general, North Wales has claimed the preference, and in certain instances, it is but justice to concede the point; while in others the usage of the South is established by good authority. The authors of our Biblical Version, have herein acted with becoming impartiality, and their example is properly regarded as the general standard.

Purity of language implies a freedom from admixture with other languages, not only as to words and phrases, but as to idiom and structure. There has been a violation of this in most parts of Wales, and even among those who ought to give an example of propriety; it being too prevailing a custom to give way to the corrupt habits of the neighbourhood. The Bards have been very jealous in this respect, but they ought not to be considered as the sole guardians of the language; the clergy ought to be equally so, especially as the style of poetry varies from that of prose, and there is a license allowed to poets, which good prose writers must not claim.

Dialect may be classed under five general heads:

1. That which effects a change in the grammatical terminations and inflections.
2. Contractions, transpositions, the omission or insertion of letters.
3. Difference of appropriation.
4. Variety of pronunciation.
5. Words used in one district and not in another.

These have been noticed in some degree by the grammarians, though nothing has been drawn up systematically on the subject. The pronunciation, with the difference in the appropriate signification of words, form the principal difficulties in colloquial intercourse: thus the Welshman of Glamorgan or Brecon, finds some difficulty at first in conversing with his countryman of Denbigh or Caernarvon: That wrong appropriation of terms, should not be charged altogether on one side as a general habit, may be ascertained by comparing the Welsh with the other Celtic languages. The instances that fall under the first head are but few; the instances of the second are numerous and mostly in South Wales; of the third class there are numerous instances, and we have already remarked. that different districts are considerably at variance in respect to pronunciation. A few examples are annexed.

1. GRAMMATICAL FORMS AND TERMINATIONS.

Lloi s. w. for *lloiau*; *tai* for *teiau*.
Tadeu, &c. for *tadau*; *caniadeu* for *caniadau*.

Efo is used in the North and *Efe* in the South.

Yrwan, or more commonly *rwan*, for *nawr*.

In the verb, we generally now say *gwrando*, &c. for *gwrandaw*. In the preter tense, in the South, they say for *rhoddodd* and *rhoddes, rhoddws*; and so in other words, but this form is found in the most ancient Bards, Taliesin and others.

In South Wales they say *para* and *gwella*, for *parhau* and *gwellhau*. They also have *gweyd* and *gwedyd* for *dweyd* and *dywedyd*; *wyf* for *ydwyf*; *yw* for *ydyw*; also *buo* for *bum*. In North Wales they are fond of the auxiliary *darfu*, as, *beth ddarfu iddo wneuthur?* There is a peculiarity in reference to the preposition. In the North they say *aeth i'w dy;* but in the South, they say *iddei dy*.

2. CONTRACTIONS & TRANSPOSITIONS.

Cwrdd for *cyfarfod*; *gwardd* for *gwahardd*.
Myntai fe for *meddau yntau*.
Bodd y chwi, for *pafodd a ydych*.
Sy for *sydd*, *wyf* for *ydwyf*.

Heddy, s. w. for *Heddyw.*
Clasgu for *casglu.*
Cwiddyl for *cywilydd.*
Pylgain for *plygain.*
Hynt for *Helynt.*
s. w. *Dy sul, Dy llun, &c.*
n. w. *Dyw sul, Dyw llun.* } *Dydd sul, &c.*

In North Wales, they are apt to insert the *i* and *y* needlessly. as in *heiddyw* for *heddyw*; *hwynt* for *hwnt*; *teidiau* for *teidau.*

In South Wales it is omitted commonly in the ending of verbs in *o*; as *neido* instead of *neidio*; *gweitho* for *gweithio*; in some nouns as *neithwr* for *neithiwr*; *dynon* for *dynion*; *heibo* for *heibio*; *gweithau* for *gweithiau.* The aspirate is commonly omitted as *waer* for *chwaer*; *wedl* for *chwedl,* and *graig* for *gwraig, grando* for *gwrando,* &c.

3. PRONUNCIATION.

The pronunciation varies considerably in different districts of both the South and North, and is much affected by the contraction of words and by the transposing of letters.

The Silurian dialect, spoken in Gwent and Glamorgan, has a peculiarity of pronunciation, which differs from all other parts of South Wales, even Brecknockshire which is so contiguous. It approaches in some instances to that of Merioneth, particularly in giving the slender sound to the vowel *a,* as in *tad, mab, cath,* &c. The plural termination of nouns is sounded exceedingly broad, as in *hadau, wiau, llafuriau,* &c. In some districts both of the North and the South, the gutturals are sounded very harshly, and the accent is prolonged by an undue emphasis, in a barbarous manner. There is also a singing tone, which prevails a good deal in Cornwall, as well as in Wales.

The radical letter is used sometimes, instead of the soft, as *map* for *mab.*

The sound of the dipthongs *ae* and *oe,* in the words *gwaed, maes, poen,* &c. in South Wales, differs from the pronunciation of North Wales; *haul* and *dau* in the former province is sounded *houl, dou,* &c. The word *bwytta* is pronounced *bytta.* The vowels *y* and *u* are confounded, in such words as *ufudd-dod, achubwr, pechaduriaid.*

South Wales generally has *ei hunan,* and *fy hunan.* North Wales is more apt to say, *ei hun, fy hun. Ym mysg* often occurs, where in the North they have *ym mhlith.*

4. WORDS USED IN ONE PROVINCE AND NOT GENERALLY IN ANOTHER.

NORTH WALES.

Go, as, go helaeth, go ddrwg.
Cyn, as, cyn wynned, cyn laned.
Tra, as, tra hynod, tra diwyd.
Odiaeth, as, melus odiaeth.
Pur, as, pur dda.
Budyr, foul.
Rhesymol, as, a ydych chwi yn rhesymol.
Namyn, as, namyn un pump ugain.
Mo, as, na ddywed mo hynny.

SOUTH WALES.

Iawnda, Pretty well.
Lled, as, Lled agos, lled dda.
Mor, as, Mor laned.

Several more examples will be found in the annexed list, containing in som-instances, the terms used in one district, with that which corresponds in another; in other instances, the one is provincial, the other general, or perhaps neither are strictly provincial, though the one may be more common than the other.

LIST OF WORDS,

Of which, the column on the left hand, comprises those more peculiar to South Wales; and the other column those which are more used in North Wales.

S. W.	N. W.
Aeth.	Arswyd.
Anferth, huge or great.	Monstrous or unshapely.
~~Arloes~~ Ar llwys.	To empty.
Bâd.	Cwch.
Baili.	Buarth.
Bera (wair neu yd).	Daes.
Blaeneu.	Mynydd-dir.
Braisg.	Prâf, Tew.
Budyr, Glam.	Cethin.
Brych, Monm.	Yn ddwys.
Ar bwys.	Yn agos.

S. W.	N. W.
Brwnt, for dirty.	Budyr.
Bron, o'r bron.	Yn rhestr.
Allwedd.	Agoriad.
Angladd.	Claddedigaeth.
Anniben.	Anhylaw.
Cann.	Peilliaid.
Carn, Dim.	Bryn.
Clwyd.	Llydiart.
Ceirios.	Sirion.
Clau.	Gwisgi.
Cymmwys.	Union.
Chwedleua.	Siarad.
Cwympo.	Syrthio.
Cyfarwydd.	Hyffordd.
	Cynefin.
Clwyf, a wound.	Clwyf, a disease.
Crynho.	Tacclus.
Crynhoi.	Ymgynnull.
Damsang.	Sathru.
Dannod.	Edliw.
Deisyf.	Dymuno.
Diofal.	Digrif.
Diwedydd, Glam.	Prydnawn.
Dihuno.	Deffro.
Dirnad.	
Dodi.	Gosod.
Ewn, Eon.	Hy.
Erfin.	Maip.
Erfyn, to expect.	Erfyn, to intreat.

S. W.	N. W.
Fald.	Buarth.
Fferem.	Tyddyn.
Ffettan.	Sach.
Ffusto.	Curo.
Ffwrn.	Pobty.
Gallt, a cliff.	Gallt, any steep.
Gwern, a swamp.	
Godechwydd, Monm.	Dusk.
Gwaith, because.	
Gwirion, quiet.	Gwirion, *non-compos*.
Girad, irad.	Alaethus.
Gyd â ni.	Efo ni.
Gwaun.	Gwairglodd.
Iawn-dda, Glam.	Gweddol.
Hynt.	Helynt.
Llafur-iau.	Yd-au.
Llechau.	Mellt.
Llaith, weak.	Llaith, moist.
Lled, prep.	
Mwrnaidd.	Mwll.
Niwl.	Tarth.
Oryg, Sil.	Darfu.
Parth.	Llawr.
Parth a.	Tuag at.
Perth.	Gwrych.
Prysur.	Difrifol.
Rhagor, addit.	Chwaneg.
Sarnu.	Trample.
Soden, a loaf.	Torth fechan.

S. W.	N. W.
Tarfu.	Dychrynu.
Tom.	Tail.
Tyle.	Rhiw.
Teisen.	
Tarfu, to scare.	Dychrynu.
Tebygu.	Tybied.
Teliaidd.	Tacclusaidd.
Trafod.	Trin.
Tre.	Cartre.
Troi tir.	Aredig.
Treisiad.	Aner.
Tyrfau.	Taranau.
Twymno.	Cynhesu.
Ysgrin.	Arch.
Yngan, to utter.	Llefaru.
Ysgadan.	Penwag-eyg.
I maes.	Allan.
I bant.	Y ffordd.

The words on the left hand of the following are more commonly used in North Wales.

Arch.	Ysgrin.
Amdo.	Amwisg.
Brâs.	Tew.
Bara gwynn.	Bara cann.

Brwd.	Gwresog.
Crybwyll.	Coffhau.
Cyn, prep.	Mor.
Dwys.	Dyfal.
Digrif.	Ysmala.
Fferri.	Sythu.
Ffynnu.	Llwyddo.
Ffynniant.	Rhwydd-deb.
Gryn (lawer).	Llaweriawn.
Gryn ofn.	Ofn mawr.
Glew.	Gwrol.
	Gwych.
Go hynod.	Lled hynod.
Hawg, yr hawg.	Ys smeityn.
Nain.	Mam gu.
Rhoddi.	Dodi.
Teulu.	Tylwyth.
Taid.	Tad cu.

With respect to the list here given, it must be observed:—1. Some of the words are not altogether restricted to one part of the principality, although they may be in more frequent use, in one district than in another. 2. We do not pretend to decide as to the use of terms and phrases, which vary in the different districts, or wish to assert that any particular word or form of expression, is wrong or to be rejected, because not much known beyond certain limits of country. It cannot be proved, that the words *Baili, Niwl, Parth, Teliaidd, Tyle, Treisiad, Ysgrin;* or, that *Cwrdd, Imaes, Diwedydd* and such like, are not genuine Welsh words, because not used in North Wales. 3. There are some instances, in which it is not so difficult to determine, as to the proper acceptation of terms; thus *Chwedleuaw,* is a better word than *Siarad;* but *Yd,* is a more proper general term than *Llafur,* for corn. *Rhynnu* is to shiver with cold, but *Sythu* means strictly to be stiffened with cold. The word *Moel* is used in North Wales, for a craggy eminence or bare top of a hill. *Twyn* is very common in South Wales, and *Garth* occurs frequently in some parts. In the North they say, *mewn difrif,* seriously; in the South, *yn brysur;* neither of these are improper. But a person who wishes to speak the language intelligibly in various parts of the country, may in many instances avoid the singular idiom of different districts, and use words which are generally understood. 4. Some words, though proper, may occur too often in discourse, as *iawn, glew, tra, cyn, go,* &c.; it may be well for writers to attend to this remark. 5. One, who writes on the theory of the language, cannot justify the use of English words, if proper Welsh words that are intelligible, can be found. Such words as *tea, brandy, coffee,* &c. being foreigners in England as well as in Wales, may be retained; unless to mend the matter, we banish the things themselves, and use our own *Llaeth, Llefrith, Cwrw da,* and *Llysiau,* instead of them. One of our recent Bards, in his admired pastorals, treats our refinements with great severity:

Crochan y felldith a'r bara gwan gwenith,
A yrrodd pob bendith a llefrith i'r llwyn,
A'r hwsmon wr esmyth, yn wan ac yn ddiffrwyth,
O'i dylwyth a'i danllwyth i dinllwyn,

As to the peculiarities of the Silurian dialect, I have noticed some of them; and for further illustration I refer to the prose extracts which I shall presently give. Most of our old Manuscripts are in this dialect, and Mr. Edward Williams has long since promised to lay before us, an Essay on the literary dialect of Gwent or Siluria.

IV. The great fault of the natives of South Wales is a want of proper attention to genuine Welsh idiom, and this is not unfrequently the case in the North. It is not sufficient, that the words be indigenous, unless the idiom correspond with the genius and structure of the language. If we make inquiry where the language is retained in greatest purity, we would refer to Merionethshire and Carnarvonshire in the North; and the hill country of Glamorgan, Monmouth and Brecon in the South, and the county of Cardigan, which has produced excellent Welshmen. Though the North boasts of being more zealously devoted to the cultivation of the Welsh language, the people of some parts of the South do not yield to them, and the latter province has produced some of the best classical Welshmen. We are now entering upon the subject of the present state of the language, and the extent of country through which it is in use. If the question be proposed, whether the language of the present age be as generally spoken in its strength and purity as in past ages, we may venture to affirm, that it is now as well understood and as generally cultivated, as it was a century ago. A certain rustic familiarity has been considered as an essential requisite of the Welsh, but that preposterous notion is wearing off; our countrymen now think and read, having various opportunities of intellectual and moral improvement, which were not enjoyed in past ages. The danger is now of over refinement, and vainly endeavouring to give our ancient tongue, a kind of varnished ornament, unsuitable to its intrinsic genius. It is well that there are respectable men, who would rather oppose than favour this novel style, which may be called by any name, and may have a few admirers, but it is not truly Cambrian, and therefore can never become popular.

We have had abundance of works translated, some of them sufficiently turgid; the persons engaged in them being seemingly much afraid, of writing with ease and simplicity, and in that perspicuous strain of composition, which at the same time is both vigorous and intelligible. But this will not justify the recent attempt at an Utopian language, whereby we have lost some of our fine English writers, by disguising rather than translating them.

The native compositions, which have appeared among us, are not numerous, and mostly or Theological subjects; among which class, a laborious work of the Rev. Thomas Charles may be mentioned with respect. As a standard of the language in original composition, we have a work entitled to the first place among the monuments of Cambrian genius, our British Lucian, the BARDD CWSG of Mr. Ellis Wynne, or The Visions of the Bard. This, was the favourite of the Rev. John Walters and Mr. Theophilus Jones.

The attempt which is now making to alter the system of orthography, which we have in the Welsh Bible, is far from being judicious; and as it has never received the sanction of public authority, but has been rather virtually rejected, it is by no means decorous to persist in imposing it on our countrymen. If philological reasons of some weight could be given, in vindication of the new system, still some deference should be paid to public opinion, before this point were pressed so strenuously; for it must tend to perplex the honest Cambrian, to meet a certain plan of orthography in one volume, and a different one in another.

The mode of Welsh orthography in common use, was not established without due regard to general propriety and public convenience: the persons who first adopted it, were men of great parts and well versed in other languages, as well as extensively acquainted with the literature of their native country, As the translators of the Bible into Welsh, established the present orthography, it was not to be supposed, that the learned Prelates appointed to be the Guardians of that important work, would admit of innovations, without being fully convinced of the necessity of a change. The reasons submitted to them some years back, were neither satisfactory to them, nor to the British and Foreign Bible Society.

I conclude this part of the subject, in the words of a learned Clergyman and an excellent Bard. "The gutturals, aspirates and plenitude of consonants, though considered an eye-sore in the new theory of vision, are nevertheless, and have been for a length of time, the appropriate and peculiar characteristics of our language. Why then should we tacitly consent to have them bartered for novel trifles, fit only to amuse and exercise the talents of a school-boy, while he is learning the rudiments of Welsh? Were I asked the question, what good would accrue to readers purely Welsh, by the adoption of the proposed alterations? My answer would be—*None*. Where the question reversed, what evil, what doubts, difficulties, &c. among the lower class; I would answer—*Much*." The same learned person applies to this subject, the reply of Dr. Johnson to some proposals of a similar nature made to that great man. "These theories may amuse a synod of philologists, but the mass of the people is too unwieldy to be governed by their *ipse dixit*."

We shall say no more at present on this article, than that in a new edition of the work of a respectable countryman, to which we have previously alluded; the system, he was so anxious to adopt while he lived, has been abandoned, and replaced by the usual plan of orthography.

V. It will be agreeable to the nature of our inquiry as to the present state of the Welsh language, to ascertain the extent of country in which it is generally spoken, and the means used in order to its cultivation. As to the first of these, there is evidence from the testimony of persons now living, or but recently deceased, that in certain neighborhoods where the Welsh obtained within the last century, it is not now spoken at all, or at least only by a few aged persons. This remark applies to Radnorshire and Monmouthshire in particular[6]; to a parish or two in Brecknockshire, and the sea coast of Glamorgan. In Montgomeryshire, on the banks of the Severn, the English is the general medium of intercourse, though in the more interior parts,

---

[6] The Welsh language is still spoken in its purity in Gwent, Uwch Coed, in that county.

the Welsh prevails. Radnorshire is completely English, at least it has lost the Welsh. A considerable part of the county of Pembroke is proverbially English, while the Northern part embracing a large population, still retains its attachment to its ancient dialect; nor does the English gain much ground on the Welsh, but rather the reverse. As to North Wales, with the exception of Montgomeryshire, which has been already mentioned, the Welsh language is generally spoken and assiduously cultivated in that country; though in some parishes of Flintshire and Denbighshire, owing to their contiguity to Chester and their intercourse with Liverpool, the Welsh is become extinct. That the Welsh language is not upon the whole in a state of declension, we may venture to affirm, though every endeavour has been made and is making to propagate the English. To diffuse among our countrymen, as far as is practicable, the knowledge of the general language of the British Empire, must be to their advantage; but let those who prefer their own ancient tongue, were it ever so inferior, and especially if it be their only language, be left to the exercise of their own judgment, and never be subjected to compulsive measures.

South Wales in general, has been regarded as more favourable to the cultivation of the English tongue, and the inhabitants not so tenacious of their ancient language; but this supposition, is not so well-founded as may at first appear; for the truth is, that though in the Towns of South Wales, English is more commonly spoken, yet in the country parishes, the attachment to the Welsh is deep-rooted.

Various means used in the last and the present age, connected with the moral culture of our countrymen, being conveyed through the medium of their language, have had the effect of producing an increased attachment to it. Improvements to a considerable extent have been made in the habits of the Cambrian peasantry; and these improvements could not have been effected, but through the medium of the language, with which the people were acquainted.

The number of books that have issued from the Welsh press, since the commencement of the present century, is highly creditable to the country; and the typographical execution of some of them evinces, that Cambrians, when they meet with encouragement, are capable of making proficiency in the civil arts.

Connected with Welsh publications, is the subject of Welsh schools, which under proper modification, deserve every support, particularly where the language is generally spoken. In the mean time, the diffusion of the English language among the rising generation, ought to have ample encouragement; but where that is not likely to answer the purpose, it must be admitted, that it will be preferable for our peasants to be instructed through the medium of their own language, rather than remain untaught and uneducated(⁷).

●●●●●●●●●●●●●●●●●●●●●●●●●●●●●●●●●●●

(⁷) Children ought not to be taught the Welsh exclusively, but be encouraged to acquire English; and where it may be desirable to be versed in both, it is preferable that they should first learn to read English.

The Bards in the present, as well as in the ages that are past, continue to be watchful guardians of Gomer's ancient tongue. They display its various powers, and as they have a wider range of subjects, and possess advantages beyond their predecessors, we have evidence to guide us in our decisions, that no age has to boast within the Cambrian regions, of sons of the *Awen*, superior to those of the nineteenth century. As we can boast then, that Cambria has a language excelling any provincial tongue in Europe; so we have among our native hills, men capable of soaring "above all vulgar height," in their intercourse with the Muse, and surpassing any of our Celtic neighbours.

VI. Taking all circumstances into our consideration, we may venture to affirm, that the language of the Cymry, once the language of Caractacus and Arthur, will never perish, though in some districts its sphere may be limited. Is it not, therefore, our best policy, to cherish native genius, and to afford our yeomen and peasants, the means of rational recreation and mental improvement? And can it be amiss for the Scholars of Cambria, whose youthful studies have been directed to the acquirement of foreign tongues, to be able to analyse and appreciate the language of their ancestors? This noble and pathetic language, has beauties worthy of the regard of those, who are acquainted with the treasures of Roman and Grecian literature. Though it is subordinate to the general language of the Empire, which is the great vehicle of the national Literature, of Law, of the Senate, and the Court, as well as the first commercial transactions; let it be treated with some respect, if it were only from a regard to what it once was, the language of our Princes and our Heroes. But it is still respectable, as the language of thousands of our countrymen, who are reputable in their stations: and if they are well versed in their own native tongue, it will be as much to their credit, as to affect an acquaintance with one which they do not understand. Let the honest Welshman, in the use of his native tongue, transact the business of life, conduct himself with decorum, acquire useful knowledge, and fulfil his duty to God and man, and why should he not be entitled to every respect?

As to what has often been said, with regard to the inconvenience of a twofold language in the same country; that will equally apply to every country, for it would be extremely convenient, if there were but one in all the world. But it is useless to regret what is inevitable, and our best mode is to improve existing circumstances to our advantage. This is the age of toleration and liberality, in which we live; let us not then be intolerant to our own ancient language, the language of our Bards, our Legislators and our Heroes, nor suffer the literature connected with it, to fall into disrepute. At the same time, while we feel we are Welshmen, we forget not that we are members of the British Empire at large; and we are sensible of the excellency of the language, which is not only that of the British Isles, but promises to be the grand medium of communication, both in the Western and Eastern world.

APPENDIX.

CONTAINING

SPECIMENS

OF

WELSH COMPOSITION,

In Prose and Verse;

WITH

MISCELLANEOUS REMARKS.

Proverbs.

PLANT gwirionedd yw hen ddiharebion.
Gwir yn erbyn y byd.
Tywyll fydd gau, goleu gwir.
Ni chêl grudd cystudd calon.

Ni chwsg Duw pan rydd ymwared.
Duw a digon, heb Dduw heb ddim.

Gair Duw goreu Dewin.
Ni thyr namyn ffol y ffydd.
Gwell angeu na chywilydd.
Gwell anian na dysg.
Gwell pwyll nac aur.
Drych i bawb ei gymmydog.
Dyn a drefna, Duw a ran.
Gwell Duw yn gâr, na llu y ddaiar.

Historical Triads.

TAIR prif ardal Ynys Prydain : Cymru, Lloegr a'r Alban.

Tair colofn gwladoldeb Ynys Prydain: Rhaith gwlad, Teyrnedd, ac Yngneidiaeth.

Translation.

OLD adages are the offspring of truth.
Truth against all the world.
Falsehood is dark, truth is clear.
The countenance cannot conceal the anguish of the heart.
God slumbers not, when he gives relief.
God is sufficient; without him, without every thing.
The word of God is the best diviner.
None but a fool will violate his faith.
Death is better than dishonour.
Genius is better than learning.
Discretion is better than gold.
Every one is a mirror to his neighbour.
Man proposes, God disposes.
God for a friend is better than a host.

Triads Translated.

THE three grand Provinces of the Isle of Britain: Cambria, Loegria and Albany, (Wales, England, Scotland).
The three Pillars of the Constitution of Britain: the Voice of the Country; the

Tri phrif Welyddon Cenedl y Cymry: y Gwenhwyson, sef gwyr Esyllwg; Gwyndydiaid, sef gwyr Gwynedd a Phowys; a Gwely Pendaran Dyfed, sef ydynt gwyr Dyfed, a Gwyr, a Cheredigiawn.

Tri Charnfradwr Ynys Prydain: Afarwy ap Lludd ab Beli Mawr, a wahoddes Ioul Caisar i'r ynys hon: Ail ydoedd Gwrtheyrn Gwrthenau, a wahoddes y Saeson gyntaf i'r Ynys hon: Trydydd y bu Medrawd, a ddug y goron oddiar Arthur, o drais a llathlud.

Tri glewion Unbennaid Ynys Prydain: Cynfelyn Wledyg, a Charadawc ap Brân, ac Arthur.

Tri Phrif lys Arthur: Caerllion ar Wysg yng Nghymru, Celliwig yng Ngherniw, a Phenryn Rhionydd yn y Gogledd.

Tri Gwesteion gwynfydedig Ynys Prydain: Dewi, Padarn a Theilaw; sef au gelwid felly, am ydd elynt yn westeion i dai Bonedd, a Gwreng, a Brodor ac Aillt,

Sovereignty, and the Decision of the Judges, (or of the Courts of Justice).

The three principal Tribes of the Cymry: the Gwentians, or the men of Siluria; the Venedotians, or the men of Gwynedd and Powys; the Clan of Pendaran of Dyved, that is the men of Dyved, or Dimetians, with those of Gower and Ceredigion, (or Cardigan).

The three arrant Traitors of Britain: Avarwy, the son of Lud, the son of Beli the Great, who invited Julius Cæsar to this Island; Gwrtheyrn or Vortigern, who gave the first invitation to the Saxons to come to this Island; Medrawd (or Modred), who through treachery and seduction deprived Arthur of his Crown.

The three gallant Sovereigns of Britain: Cunobelin, Caradoc the son of Bran, and Arthur.

The three Palaces of Arthur: Caerleon upon Usk, Gelliwyg in Cornwall, and Penrhyn Rionydd in the North.

The three blessed Visitants: Dewi, Padarn, and Teilaw, (David, Paternus, and Teliaus), who were so called, because they visited the houses of the Gentry and the heb gymmeryd na rhodd na gwobr, na bwyd na llyn; eithr dysgu y Ffydd yng Nghrist y wnaent i bawb, heb na thâl na diolch, eithr i dlawd ac anghenus y rhoddynt roddion o'u haur, a'u gwisgoedd a'u bwydydd.

Moral Maxims in the form of Triads, called
TRIOEDD CADOC DDOETH.

TRI pheth a gaiff y gwallus; cywilydd, colled, a gwatwar.
Tri pheth a gaiff y difalch; amlder, llawenydd a chariad ei gymmydogion.

Tri pheth a gaiff y cywir; dawn, parch a ffyniant.
Tri pheth a gaiff anghywir; byd drwg, gair drwg, a diwedd drwg.

Tri sail doethineb; synwyr i ddysgu, cof i gado, a chymendawd i adrawdd.

Tri pheth gwell no chyfoeth; iechyd, rhyddid a synwyr.
Tri pheth a gaiff dyn wrth ymgyfreithio; cost, gofal a thrafferth.

Commonality, Aliens and Natives, without receiving either gift or reward, or meat or drink; and they communicated instruction in the Christian Faith to all people, free of all remuneration, distributing also, money, food and raiment, to the poor and the necessitous.

Moral Maxims Translated.

THREE things attend the careless: shame, loss, and derision.

The three acquisitions of the lowly: plenty, cheerfulness, and the love of his neighbours.

The three acquisitions of rectitude: endowment, honour, and prosperity.

The three attendants of dishonesty: to be in bad circumstance, to have a bad word, and to come to a bad end.

The three foundations of wisdom: capacity to acquire, memory to retain, and promptitude to impart.

There are three things better than riches: health, freedom, and understanding.

Three things are the consequence of going to law: expence, anxiety, and trouble.

Tri pheth a ennillant enw da i ddyn; gwedyd ychydig, gwneuthur daioni, ac ym-
lafuriaw.

---

*From Brut y Brenhinoedd, or the Chronicle of
the Kings of Britain.*

PRYDAIN oreu o'r ynysoedd, yr hon a
elwyt gynt y WEN YNYS, yngorllewinol
eigiawn rhwng Ffraingc a'r Iwerddon y mae
gosodedic; wyth cant milltir y sydd yn y
hyt, a deu cant yn y lled: a pheth bynnac
a fo rhaid i dynawl arfer, o anniffyge-
dig ffrwythlonder, hi a wasanaetha ygyt
hynny. Cyflawn o bob cenedl mwyn a
metael, hefyd ffrwythlawn yw o maesdiredd
llydan amyl, a bryneu arderchog addas, i
dir diwyllodraeth, trwy y rheu ydeuant
amryfaelon genedloedd frwytheu yndi.
Hevyt y maent coedydd a llwyneu, cyflawn
o amgen genedloedd aniveilieit, a bwyst-
vileit. Ac or diwedd pymp cenedlaeth y
sydd yn y chyfaneddu hi; nyd amgen Nor-
manneit, Brytanyeit, a Saesson, a Ffichdeit,
ac Ysgotiaid.

Three things that procure a man a good name: to be sparing of his words, to practise what is good, and to be diligent in labour.

Translation.

BRITAIN, the first of Islands, formerly styled the White (or Fair Island): situated between France and Ireland in the Western ocean. Eight hundred miles is the extent thereof, and the breadth two hundred, and is inexhaustible in every production requisite for the use of man. It abounds with every kind of mines, and with numerous and extensive plains; the hills are high and lofty, and the soil well adapted to tillage. It produces very great abundance, of every kind of grain, and the choicest fruits. The woods and forests abound with a variety of animals, and afford pasturage for cattle. It is now inhabited by five different nations; Britons, Saxons, Normans, Picts, and Scots.

The Welsh Bible.

THE New Testament was translated into Welsh, by Mr. Wm. Salisbury of Llansannan, Denbighshire, he being assisted by Dr. Richard Davies, and Dr. Morgan, in the completion of the work. The latter Gentleman was the principal person engaged in translating the Old Testament, and he as well as Dr. Davies, were deservedly raised to the Episcopal bench. The New Testament came forth in the year 1567, and the whole of the Scriptures about 1588. The Primate Dr. Whitgift, gave every encouragement to the undertaking. It is upon the whole an excellent Version, and in some passages superior to the English; the work in general, evinces the persons engaged in it to be men of great learning and ability, and proves the language to be capable, of well sustaining the important subjects contained in it. We may observe, that in some places, it accords more with the translation in use in the sixteenth century, than with that of King James. It afterwards received a revision from Bishop Parry, and how far that extended as to the interpretation of particular texts, can only be ascertained by a careful collation of Dr. Morgan's version, with that corrected by Parry, assisted by the learned Dr. John Davies, the lexicographer. Our Welsh translators, may be pronounced more free from Calvinian prejudices, than the authors of King James's version, and the sense of the Original is generally well expressed by appropriate Welsh language.

"This translation, says Mr. Walters, is remarkable for the purity of the language, and a native simplicity of style which so eminently characterises the original; for it hath been observed by the skilful in both languages, that there is a surprizing affinity between the *Hebrew* and the *Ancient British*, in their idioms, peculiarities of style, and mod or turn of expression." *Walter's Dissertation.*

It possesses an advantage, in not abounding with the obsolete terms, which are found in our authorized English Bible; although it would still admit of some improvement, partly as to rendering the sense more obvious, and the style more easy and free.

Extract from the Mabinogion, or, Welsh Fairy Tales. Cambr. Register, Vol. III.

Pwyll yntau, Pen Annwn, a ddaeth i'r berllan, ar ei ganved marchog, val y gorchymynasai Rianon ito, ac y gôd ganto; a gwisgaw bratau trymion ymdano a wnaeth, a llopanau mawr am ei draed. A phan wybu ei bod ar dechreu cyvetach, wedi bwyta, dawed rhacdo i'r cyntet; ac wedi ei dawed i'r neuadd, cyvarch gwell a wnaeth i Wawl vab Clud, ac ei gyd ymdeithon o wyr a gwreiget.

"Duw a roto da it, a gresaw Duw wrthyt!" hebai Gwawl vab Clud.

"Arglwyt, y nev a dalo it! negesawl wyf wrthyt," heb yntau.

"Gresaw wrth dy neges," hebai Gwawl; ac os arch gyvartal a erchi imi, yn llawen ti ai cefi.

"Cyvartal arglwyt, heb yntau: nid archav onid rhac eiseu: sef arch a archav, llonaid y gôd vechan a weli dy o vwyd."

"Arch didrahaus hono, a thi a'i cefi yn

Translation.

Pwyll, Chief of Annwn, came also into the orchard, with his hundred Knights, agreeably to the instructions of Rianon, having the bag with him, clad in wretched rags and large clogs on his feet. So when he knew the carousal was to begin, he approached the hall, and having entered the portal, he addressed himself to Gwawl, the son of Clud, and to his company both male and female.

" May God increase thy store, and may he grant thee his favour," said Gwawl the son of Clud.

" My Lord, may Heaven requite thee! I am a suitor to thee," was the reply.

" Welcome to thy suit," said Gwawl;" "and if reasonable be thy request, gladly shalt thou have it."

" Reasonable, my Lord," the other rejoined; "I crave only to supply my want: this is the boon I ask, as much victuals as will fill this small bag."

" No exorbitant request that, and thou

llawen—Dygwch fwyd itto, hebai Gwawl vab Cludd.

Rhivedi mawr o swytwyr a gyvodasant i vynyt, a dechreu llenwi y gôd; ac er a vynid ynti, ni vytai llawnach no chynt.

"Enaid!" llevai Gwawl, "a vyt llawn dy gôd ti byth!"

"Na vyt, ar vy nghydwybod," heb yntau, "er a doter ynti byth, oni chyvyt dylyedawctir a daiar a chyvoeth, a sengi a'i deutroed y bwyd yn y gôd, a dywedyd, "digon a doded yma.

"A genad, cyvod i vynyt ar vyr," hebai Rhianon, wrth Wawl vab Clud.—"Cyvodav yn llawen," hebai ev.

Cyvodi i vynyt a oruc, a dodi ei deutroed yn y gôd. Yna troi o Pwyll ynivyt Gwawl tros ei ben ynti; ac yn gyvlym cau y gôd, a llat clwm ar y careuau, Pwyll a dodes lev ar ei gorn. Ac ar hynny, llyma y teulu am ben y llys. Yna cymmeryd o Bwyll bawb o'r niver a daeth ygyda Gwawl, ac eu dodi yn ei garchar ei hun.

shalt have it, with pleasure. Carry victuals to him," said Gwawl the son of Clud.

A great number of the attendants then rose up, and so began to fill the bag; but after all that was put in, it seemed no fuller for it.

"Good man!" exclaimed Gwawl, "will thy bag never be full?"

"It will not upon my conscience," the other replied, "for all that may be put in, unless a Chieftain, possessed of dominion, shall tread the victuals in the bag with his feet, and say, there has been enough put in."

"Thou hast leave," said Rianon, speaking to Gwawl, "rise up without delay;

"I will rise with pleasure," he replied.

So he rose and put his two feet in the bag. Then Pwyll turned up the bag in a way that Gwawl was over his head therein; and dexterously shutting it, by slipping a knot on the thongs, Pwyll gave a blast with his horn. In the mean time, Pwyll took the retinue of Gwawl and put them into prison.

Extracts from the Laws of Howel, *&c..*

Tri anghyvarch gwr; ei farch ai arfau, ac a ddel iddo o'i dir; ac a ddel yn wyneb warth gan ei wraig am ei chowyll: ni ddyly yntau rannu un o hynny a'i wraig. *Trioedd Cyvraith.*

O dervydd i ddyn caffael cig anifel ni bai eiddo ei hun, ai gan gwn, ai yng nguddfa, a'i gymmeryd heb gennad Arglwydd o hono; dirwy a wg fydd, hyd ydd el, nag o rodd, nag o bryn, nag o waddawl, hyd y ganfed law; wrth hynny gelwir hwnnw, cyhyryn canastyr, ac nid aa bellach na hynny. *Cyvraith Hywel.*

Tri phriodolder y sydd i bob dyn; rhyw, a braint ac etifeddiaeth: etifeddiaeth hagen herwydd braint, braint herwydd rhyw, rhyw herwydd y gwahan a vydd rhwng dynion herwydd cyfraith; megis y gwahan brenin a breyr, breyr a bilain, gwr a gwraig, hynav a ieuav. *Trioedd Cyvraith.*

Clust vab Clustveinad; deg milltir a deugaint y clywai y morgrugyn y bore, pan gychwynai y ar ei nyth. *Mabinogion.*

Tair sarhaed ni ddiwygir, or cefir trwy feddwdod; sarhaed yr offeiriad teulu, a'r yngad llys, a'r meddyg teulu; can ni wyddant hwy py amser y bo raid i'r brenin wrthynt; ni ddylyant wyntau vod yn veddw byth. *Cyfraith Hywel.*

From Bardd Cwsg, *or the Visions of the Bard.*

The introduction to the third Vision, is considered a beautiful specimen of composition, and as such it is here presented to the reader.

Ar foreu têg o Ebrill rywiog, a'r ddaear yn lâs feichiog, a Phrydain baradwysaidd, yn gwisgo lifrai gwychion, arwyddion *Heulwen Hâ;* rhodio yr oeddwn ynglan *Hafren,* ynghanol melysbyncieu cerddorion bach y goedwig, oedd yn ymryson torri pob mesurau mawl hyfrydlais i'r Creawdwr; a minnau 'n llawer rhwymediccaeh, weithieu mi gyd byngciwn a'r cor ascellog mwynion, ac weithieu darllenwn ran o lyfr *Ymarfer Duwioldeb.* Er hynny yn y myw, nid ac o'm cof fy ngweledigaethau o'r blaen, na redent fyth a hefyd i'm rhwystro, ar draws pob meddyliau eraill. A daliasant i'm blino, nes immi wrth fanwl ymresymmu, ystyried nad oes un weledigaeth ond oddiuchod, er rhybudd i ymgroesi; ac wrth hynny, fod arnai ddyled iw sgrifennu hwynt i lawr, er rhybudd i eraill hefyd. Ac ar ganol hynny o waith, a mi yn bendrist yn ceisio casglu rhai o'r cofion ofnadwy, daeth arnai heppian uwchben fy mhappur, a hynny a roes le i fy Meistr *Cwsg*, lithro ar fy ngwartha.

No. II.

Remarks on Orthography.

DIFFERENT plans of orthography have been in use among the Welsh, in different ages, but none upon the whole, can suit public convenience better, than that which is used in our Biblical version, and which has therefore the sanction of public authority. The different impressions have varied a little as to the accommodation in spelling proper names, and some things of minor importance; but great care has been taken in the late Oxford editions, to regulate the orthography of the Welsh, still adhering to the general system long recognized. The gentlemen, who exerted themselves on that occasion, were persons possessed of an adequate judgment for the task imposed upon them; and by deliberately attending to the work, they had opportunity of discriminating the proper mode of procedure. But for any unauthorized individual, to introduce a novel system, is the way to bring about much confusion, and it must be far better to bear with alleged defects, than to palm novelties upon the public, maugre the well known objections that have been repeatedly urged. Utility ought to be the first consideration, and ornamental appearance only secondary; but where can be the utility, of making a sweeping change, that would have the effect with many of a revolution in the language? But this new system of characters, is also accompanied with an innovation in the style of composition, which destroys all our old established notions of propriety. The defects of the English alphabet are not trivial, when viewed in the abstract, and many a pedant may propose very sapient alterations, but currency and use have stamped that authority on the present system, which is not likely to be soon abandoned. "All attempts," says Dr. Llewelyn, "to change letters once introduced, though in many instances wrong and defective, have yet been generally ineffectual."

That one simple character should be used to express one sound, would at first view appear exceedingly just and proper, but there are reasons that prevent this being practicable in other European languages, as well as the Welsh. To attempt that refinement in a provincial, which it is not thought worth contending for in a great national language, is certainly incongruous. But it may be argued, that if in a few instances, an improvement is practicable, why should not a change for that purpose be adopted ; as in substituting the single F, for the double one and the V, instead of the former letter. This, however, would to some persons bear an uncouth aspect, and you might as well do away with all the double characters, and in particular the Dd, which is liable to as great an objection as any character, and was at one time more properly expressed by Dh, answering to the soft Th, in English words.

The doubling of certain letters merely for the sake of sound, when the etymology or derivation does not require it, is exploded by some of our philologists; but others, exclaim against the affected rejection of the usual mode, and do not choose to be governed by a more novel plan as not being in conformity with the genius of the language, and the plain habits of the people who speak it. As to unseemly aspect, the present Welsh orthography as well as the system of etymology, is superior to that of the Gaelic, the Manks and the Breton; and as the Welsh community are a plain people, we must content ourselves with utility rather than refinement.

No. III.

Style of Welsh writers.

MOST of our modern prose compositions are translations from the English, and many of these performances done in such a way as to prove, that the persons engaged, either did not understand their authors, or had no ability to write, with force and clearness, in their native tongue. Translating is not so easy a task, as some may be apt to conceive, and has difficulties pertaining to it, which do not attend original composition. This will particularly hold good, in reference to Welsh translations, which seldom express an author's meaning with clearness, in an easy flowing diction. Some works are very unsuitable for this purpose, and others which might be rendered suitable with a little accommodation, are spoiled for want of skill and attention in the translator.

The short specimens of Welsh given in these papers, will serve to display the difference, between the style of our ancestors, and modern Welsh writers. We are not required to adopt all their phrases, while in many things we may perceive a propriety and fitness in their expressions, far more congenial to pure language, than those in present use.

I shall here subjoin extracts, from the Commentary of the late Rev. Peter Williams, as a specimen of good writing.

Matth. xviii. Gallwn sylwi, fod hunan ym mhawb, a dirgel chwennychiad am anrhydedd; ac mae 'n debyg mai gwreiddyn yr ymholi a wnaeth y disgyblion yn eu plith eu hunain, ac wrth ein Iachawdwr, ynghylch pwy fyddai fwyaf, oedd y dyb gamsyniol (cyffredin ym mysg yr Iuddewon) fod y Messia i osod i fynu lywodraeth wledyg.

Ephes. vi. Y mae 'r dyledswyddau teuluaidd, a orchymynir yn nechreu y bennod, yn haeddu eu hystyried yn dda, gan bawb a ewyllysiant ddaioni i'r wladwriaeth, a llwyddiant yr eglwys; canys y mae teuluwriaeth crefyddgar, ac ymddygiad bucheddol, ym mysg tylwyth, megis hâdle ffrwythlon, neu wyddlan araul, lle y tyf planhigion peraidd, a choed defnyddgar at ddodrefn, arddwriaeth ac adeiladaeth.

The following extract is submitted to the judgment of the reader.

Pregeth ar Dduwdod ein Iachawdwr, gan y Parchedig Dr. Coke. Cyfieithad, J. H.

Dilynwch nattur, os gellwch chwi, trwy ei holl effeithiau a'i hymddangosiadau nes i chwi ddinoethi ei phrif wyddorion hi. A fedrwch chwi amgyffred y modd, y tyf y glaswelltyn allan o'r ddaear? A fedrwch chwi amgyffred a deongli, nattur yr undeb rhwng corph marwol ac yspryd anfarwol? Os methwn amgyffred pethau creedigol, pa rhyfedd os methwn amgyffred ein Creaw- dwr? Pa fodd y dichon y meidrol a'r terfynedig, amgyffred y bod anfeidrol?

Yr ysgrythyrau yn unig, a roddant i ni ddatguddiad addas a chyfiawn o Dduw, ai ewyllys. Ein dyledswydd ni yw derbyn, *la. Abertawy 'Argraffedig yn Swyddfa Seren Gomer, gan J. Harris, dros Gymmdeithas Anrhydeddus y Gymmreigyddion, 1822, Gwerth Chwe'cheiniog. Yn syd rhwyfin a Amcanion .. Cymdeithas 77 Hedwch....., Abertawe.. Chast Nes.   Abertawe.. J. Harris, 1822.*

yr hyn a fynegant hwy, am yr Hanfod dwyfol, gyd â'r parch a'r gostyngeiddrwydd mwyaf, er fod gwirioneddau ynddynt, y rhai ydynt uwchlaw cyrhaeddiad rheswm dynol, er nad ydynt yn gwrthwynebu rheswm.

The above extracts, both as to style and orthography, belong to *the old school*; but for a more novel, and some may think, a more elegant mode, I refer to Dr. Owen Pugh's COLL GWYNVA, or Translation of Milton's Paradise Lost. An Address[1] delivered by Mr. Griffith Jones of Dolgelley, before the Gwyneddigion Society in London, expressed in the style and manner to which I allude, is recommended to the attention of the ingenious Cambrian. It is certainly desirable, that a more happy and pleasing manner of both speaking and writing the language should obtain, than what has been the general practice, and it would be well for the pulpit orators in old Cambria, to pay some regard to Mr. Griffith Jones's suggestions, though the new

1. *Araeth Mr. Griffith Jones, (Dolgellau) Llywydd y Cymreigyddion, Ysgrifenydd y Gwyneddigion, A Rhodd Cymdeithas y Bwrdd Crwn, O'r Gadair, gan Gwydd Cymdeithas y Gymreigyddion*

style might not be deemed altogether suitable for public addresses. Surely a middle path may be found, and indeed it has been already traced by many respectable individuals; avoiding the opposite extremes of vulgarity and pedantry. Should it be deemed preposterous for a plain Welshman to affect Ciceronian elegance, yet no excuse can be made for offering outrage to common decency.

Mr. Griffith Jones, in his address to his countrymen, laments the general want of attention to good speaking and elegant diction among Welshmen. This, he pleads, is not owing to any defect in the language, the reverse of which he himself is a happy instance. I shall give an extract or two:
"Nad yw areithio yn yr Iaith Gymraeg, yn cael ei goleddu yn fwy cyffredinol—iaith nad oes ei phereiddiach, nac ei grymmusach mewn geiriau, nac ei chadarnach mewn ymadrodd, nac un mwy galluog i weithredu ar feddyliau dynion, ac i amlygu eu gwahanol deimladau, pa un ai llawenydd neu dristwch, poen neu hyfrydwch, cariad neu ddigter, canmoliad neu achwyniad, yn

byd—sydd achos o syndod, ac weithiau o dristwch i mi."

The advice given towards the conclusion of the address, is worthy the regard of all, who use the Welsh language in public: "Terfynaf, gan erfyn arnoch ymgeisio yn wastadol, i amlygu eich meddyliau mewn geiriau addas at yr amgylchiad: os difrifol y testyn, bydded eich ymadrodd felly: hefyd, os godidog, gochelwch ciriau gwael a gwammal: os ysgafn, bydded eich dywediadau yn ys gafn hefyd. Bydded eich cymhariaethau, a'ch darluniadau, bob amser yn addas i'r gwrthddrych yn eich golwg."

The instances selected from the Bards by Mr. Jones, by way of illustration, are here annexed, as suitable to our design:

 Er trallod, er cryndod, er cri—yn oer ing,
 Yn awr angau difri;
 Yn nydd barn gadarn gwedi,
 Duw tad na ymad â mi.
    R. Jones.

 Y nos dywell yn dystewi—caddug,
 Yn cuddio 'r Eryri;

A'r haul yn ngwely 'r heli,
A'r lloer yn ariannu 'r lli.
Parch. W. Davies.

———Digofaint dygyfor,
Lle bo mellt yn lleibio mor;
Pob glyn, pob dyffryn, pob dôl,
Dinasoedd yn dân ysol;
Yn llwyr ddifa gyrfa gaeth,
Degwch y gre'edigaeth.
Cywydd y Farn gan R. Jones.

In concluding this subject, I beg leave to say to those who wish to render themselves both useful and agreeable: that rusticity is not a necessary concomitant of our native dialect; that it is capable of a neat, flowing and expressive manner. We should notice its own peculiar idioms, in connexion with the general rules of good composition, and the general circumstances of the community. In avoiding puerility of diction, we must not affect a turgid and bombastic manner; nor give that uncommon turn to our expressions, nor novel terminations to words, which would carry a strange sound to the ears of the generality of our countrymen. The Welsh language is well adapted for the florid style, and an occasional turn of that kind, may be agreeable, as in the second specimen from Mr. Peter Williams; but much of it obscures the style and shows a want of good judgment. We may here form a Triad; There are three requisites of good composition, The first of which is, to understand our subject; The second is to render it intelligible to others; The third is to use a style of expression, that comprizes purity, force and attraction.

As to those ingenious men who wish to try their skill in polishing our old language, as a matter of curiosity, and to set it up as a rival of a great national language; to them we would say, that general utility is to be preferred to any plausible scheme of ingenious trifling. We would wish to recommend a style and manner of writing of the most simple structure, with a degree of elevation when the subject requires it; but to abjure as much as possible all the *Verba sesquipedalia* of both old and modern authors. The style of BARDD CWSG, though elegant and rather florid, does not violate this maxim. The following description of the requisites of a good war-horse, would not do for frequent imitation:

Cad-farch, cadarn-dew, cerdded-ddrud, llydan-gefn, hron-eang, gast-gyfyng, carn-gragen, ymdeith-wastad, hywedd falch, drythyll, llamsachus, ffroen ffol, a'i lygad yn frith las dratheryll."

The facility of the Welsh language for forming compounds should be but sparingly used, especially by ordinary prose writers; as to the Poets, we do not take upon us to say any thing to them on the subject. Good sense, sound judgment, and an acquaintance with the properties of the language, will best serve to direct the writer, and preserve him from the errors, which would prove both injurious to his credit, and hinder the pleasure and profit of the reader.

WELSH POETRY.

There are twenty-four Canons of Welsh versification which consist of nine GORCHANAU or primary principles, and the combinations of these are called ADLAWIAID or secondaries, in number fifteen. According to the ancient system, called Dosparth Morganwg, these were very scientifically arranged, but the supposed improvement more generally adopted since the famous Session of Bards, held at Carmarthen in the reign of King Edward the fourth, does not possess the same beautiful simplicity. The superiority of the more ancient system is now admitted by our Classical Bards, and the question decided by the Rev. Walter Davies, in his masterly Essay on the subject. To the laws and principles of Cambrian song, the following Triads are applicable:

1. The three requisities of versification: metricity, consonancy and rhyme.

2. The three properties of metre: the length of the line, the form of the stanza, and the power of the accent.
3. The three primary distinctions of metre: the Cowydd, the Englyn and the Awdl.
4. The three excellencies of metre: correctness, freedom and harmonious accent.
5. The three varieties of verse: variation of metricity, variation of consonancy, and variation of accent.
6. The three primary principles of cynghanedd or consonancy: the rhyming consonancy, the alliterative consonancy, and the compound consonancy of rhyme and alliteration.

1. Tri anhepcor mydryddiaeth: colofn, cynghanedd ac awdl.
2. Tri phriodoldeb mesur: hyd y ban, dull y pennill, a phwys yr accan.
3. Tri phrifrywiogaeth ar vesur: cowydd, ynglyn ac awdl.
4. Tri rhagoriaeth mydyr: cywreindeb, rhwyddineb, ac accan bêr.
5. Tri amrywiaeth ban: amrywiaeth cyhydedd, amrywiaeth cynghanedd, ac amrywiaeth accan.
6. Tair cynghanedd sydd o brif ansawdd: cynghanedd sain, cynghanedd groes, a chynganedd lusg.

"The English reader, to use the words of Mr. Walters, may be able to form some faint idea, some imperfect notice of the singularity of the Welsh language in the formation or construction of its poetical numbers, from the following stanza on Envy:

> A Fiend in Phœbus' fane he found,
> That yonder grew, yet under ground,
> Sprung from the spawn of spite;
> The elf his spleen durst not display,
> Nor act the Devil in the day,
> But at the noon of night.

The following instances of alliteration from Virgil, noticed by Mr. Walter Davies, are curious:

" Hinc exaudiri voces et verba vocantis Visa viri."

" Neu patriæ validas in viscera vertite vires."

Horace and Anacreon abound with instances of the same kind. The very first Ode of the former, and the first also in the latter, are in illustration of the point in hand.

By the nine *Gorchanau*, or canons of metricity, are understood so many varieties of lengths or numbers of syllables in a verse, including from four to twelve syllables, being adequate to every possible change that can be used agreeable to the laws of harmony. The names of these elements of metre are as follows:

Cyhydedd
- Fer,   Syll. 4. Short.
- Gaeth,   5. Confined.
- Drosgl,   6. Rugged.
- Lefn,   7. Smooth.
- Wastad,   8. Regular.
- Draws,   9. Cross.
- Wen,   10 Flowing.
- Laes,   11. Heavy.
- Hir,   12. Long.

The *Adlawiaid*, secondary or compound principles, being fifteen in number, are all the possible variety of combinations of the *Gorchanau*, depending upon the different lengths or quantity and rhyme; the first arising from a junction of unequal verses; and the latter from changes or variety of rhyme: the names are—

Ban cyrch.	Recurrent pause.
Toddaid.	Confluency.
Triban milwr.	Warrior's triplet.
Triban cyrch.	Recurrent triplet.
Cowydd.	Recitative.
Traethodyn.	Compound Recitative.
Proest cadwynawdl.	Combined alternate rhyme.
Proest cyfnewidiawg.	Combined vowel alternity.
Clogyrnach.	Rugosity.
Hupynt.	Vaulting strain.
Llamgyrch	Recurrent transition.
Cadwyn gyrch.	Recurrent catenation.
Ynglyn.	Continuity.
Cynghawg.	Complexity.
Dyri.	Unconnected quantity.

Some of the above names are not found in the recent Catalogues of the 24 Metres, and others are placed instead of them. Thus the *Triban* is omitted, and we have *Gorchest y Beirdd*, and instead of the generic term *Cynghawg*, we have *Gwawdodyn byr a*

www.ingramcontent.com/pod-product-compliance
Lightning Source LLC
Chambersburg PA
CBHW030341230426
43664CB00007BA/492